Field Guide to
BUTTERFLIES

Based on
The Butterfly Guide
by W. J. Holland, LL.D.

With photographs by
Steven Daniel
Carol A. Southby
David T. Southby

A MAIN STREET BOOK

Text for this book was adapted and updated from
The Butterfly Guide
© 1915 by W. J. Holland

Photography by
Steven Daniel, Carol A. Southby, and David T. Southby

Editor: Cassia B. Farkas
Design and production: Alan Barnett, Inc.

10 9 8 7 6 5 4 3 2 1

Library of Congress Cataloging-in-Publication Data available upon request

© 2003 by Sterling Publishing Co., Inc.
Published by Sterling Publishing Co., Inc.
387 Park Avenue South, New York, NY 10016
Distributed in Canada by Sterling Publishing
c/o Canadian Manda Group, One Atlantic Avenue, Suite 105
Toronto, Ontario, Canada M6K 3E7
Distributed in Great Britain by Chrysalis Books
64 Brewery Road, London N7 9NT, England
Distributed in Australia by Capricorn Link (Australia) Pty. Ltd.
P.O. Box 704, Windsor, NSW 2756, Australia

Manufactured in China
All rights reserved

Sterling ISBN 1-4027-0693-6

CONTENTS

5
Preface

7
Introduction

25
The Species

211
Glossary

213
Index

Preface

by Jacqueline B. Glasthal

To the literary world, Vladimir Nabokov gained fame as the Russian-born author of *Lolita*. But to the scientific community, surprisingly enough, he is remembered just as well—if not better—for his expertise as a lepidopterist. And when it came to butterfly research, one of his most oft-used resources was a 1933 edition of W. J. Holland's *The Butterfly Book*, extensively marked up with his own handwritten notes throughout.

Of course our knowledge of butterflies—and the classification systems used by experts studying them—has changed greatly since Holland and Nabokov shared with readers their passion for these "winged fairies of the woods and fields" (as Holland called them). Indeed, the science of zoology is one that, like butterflies themselves, seems to require occasional metamorphoses in its attempts to reveal its truest self. Thus, in updating and bringing out this metamorphosis of Holland's classic work, originally published in 1898, the editors walked a fine line between preserving the best of Holland's scientific manual, lauded in its day for its clarity and accessibility to laypeople, while at the same time modernizing it to reflect the most up-to-date research available on the subject today.

Back in Holland's time, for example, scientists had no knowledge of how butterflies use their genetic circuitry to turn on enzymes that produce the pigments responsible for wing decoration. Neither did they have microchips to help track the flight patterns of Monarchs and other butterflies. Even more to the point, especially for the purposes of this field guide, close-focusing binoculars and cameras with zoom lenses were not readily available. Today, no longer must amateur naturalists who feel compelled to "capture" proof of their sightings rely solely on butterfly nets and specimen boxes to bring their discoveries home. For many, a set of detailed photographs will suffice, while the subjects of their admiration, affection, and fascination are thus allowed to remain out and about in their natural habitat, contributing to nature's cycles.

In this version of the book we have updated and edited—but rarely enlarged upon—Holland's writing. As you will see, he was not particularly loquacious, instead inviting readers to allow his "figures"—the plates that appeared throughout his book—to "speak" for themselves. He was particularly proud that his field guide was able to avail itself of 3-color printing, a cutting edge technology at the time. Now, thanks to further advances in print technology and modern photography, we have enhanced Holland's text and illustrations even more with detailed, color-accurate photos throughout.

In our effort to pay much-deserved homage to Holland and his classic work, we have chosen to retain his original layout and arrangement of species. However, all scientific names used herein conform to those accepted and recognized by the North American Butterfly Association (NABA) at our time of publication. You will thus find within these pages Holland's family and subfamily descriptions, as well as a table of the families and subfamilies currently used by NABA, allowing you to compare and contrast the two. Note though, that even among today's lepidopterists, there are hotly-debated points of contention as to correct classification. Given that, we have simply done our best to reach a consensus among our own experts.

William Jacob Holland (1848–1932) was, in many ways, a remarkable man. Not only was he known to have the largest and most comprehensive butterfly collection in North America. (This book in its day was regarded as the classic on the subject, containing a description of every butterfly on the North American continent that was known at the time.) He excelled in other sciences and subjects as well. He was one of the world's first authorities on paleontology, and dug up an 84-foot-long dinosaur in Wyoming in 1898, the largest fossil of its kind found until that time. In addition to *The Butterfly Book*—this volume's original title—Dr. Holland also authored *The Moth Book* (1903), *To the River Plate and Back* (1913), *The Butterfly Guide* (1915), and many scientific papers published by the United States government, the Zoological Society of London, and similar official scientific publishers.

Every attempt possible was made in this field guide to honor both the old and the new, given the constraints and restrictions with which we were presented. But even with this book's challenges and its ultimate limitations, we hope that it will serve you well, helping you to identify and better appreciate those butterflies you are most likely to spot in your outdoor meanderings through woods, fields, and perhaps even your own backyard—while at the same time offering you a glimpse back to the way butterflies were looked at, perceived, and thought about in an earlier, simpler time.

Introduction

THE PLACE OF BUTTERFLIES IN THE ANIMAL KINGDOM

The Animal Kingdom is divided into various subkingdoms. One of these is the subkingdom of the *Arthropoda*. The word is derived from the Greek nouns *arthron* meaning joint, and *pous* meaning foot.

The *Arthropoda* have bodies composed of a series of rings, tubes, or segments jointed together by flexible skin, and organs made up of tubular sections joined in a similar way. Arthropods are invertebrates; they do not have backbones and internal skeletons, as do fish, reptiles, birds, and mammals—including man—who have endoskeletons, or "inside skeletons," with muscles clothing the bones. In arthropods the hard parts clothe the muscles, they have exoskeletons, or "outside skeletons," and control their movements by muscles that pull from the inside.

The subkingdom of the *Arthropoda* is divided into six classes, one of which consists of the *Insecta* (insects). The class *Insecta* is subdivided into many orders, and butterflies belong to the order *Lepidoptera*, having two sub-orders: the *Rhopalocera*, or butterflies, and the *Heterocera*, or moths. Both are characterized by having scaly wings, hence the name, derived from the Greek words *lepis* meaning scale, and *pteron* meaning wing. *Lepidoptera* are "scale-winged insects." Anyone who has ever handled a butterfly or moth will have noticed a dust-like substance rubs off from the wings, which under a microscope is seen to be composed of minute scales (see Plate A, Fig. a). Looking at the wing of a butterfly under a magnifying glass reveals that it is covered with such scales, arranged like the scales on a fish, or the shingles on a roof (see Plate A, Fig. b).

Butterflies are mainly diurnal in their habits, preferring the sunshine. Most moths, on the other hand, are nocturnal, and fly in the dusk or after dark. Butterflies are therefore often called *diurnal Lepidoptera*, and moths are spoken of as *nocturnal Lepidoptera*.

Ordinarily, the best way to distinguish between butterflies and moths is by examining their antennæ. In the case of butterflies, the antennæ are thread-like terminating in a small knob-like, or club-like enlargement. It is this fact which has led naturalists to call them *Rhopalocera*. The word is derived from the Greek nouns *rhopalon* meaning a club, and *keras* a horn. Butterflies are *Lepidoptera* that have clubs at the end of their antennæ, which may be short, long, or hooked (see Plate A, Figs. g, h, i). The forms seen in the antennæ of moths are very various. Moths are therefore known as *Heterocera*, from the Greek adjective *hetero* meaning all sorts, and the noun *keras* a horn.

THE ANATOMY OF BUTTERFLIES

The body of a butterfly consists of the head, the thorax, and the abdomen (see Plate A, Fig. c).

The head carries two relatively large eyes, one on either side. The eyes of insects are compound, and if examined under a microscope are seen to have many minute facets, which serve to gather the light from all directions, so that butterflies can look forward

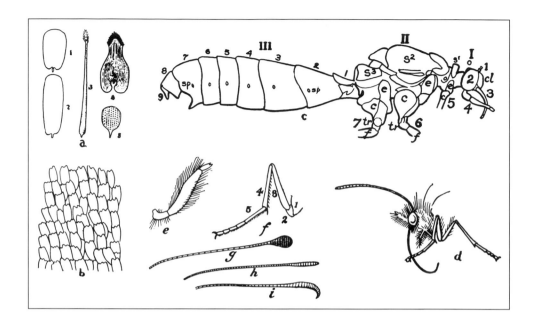

PLATE A

Fig. a. *Magnified scales of butterflies.* 1, ordinary scale of *Papilio*; 2, do. of *Colias*; 3, *androconium*, or scale from wing of male *Megista, cymela* (Little Wood-Satyr); 4, do. of male *Pieris napi* (Mustard White); 5, do. of male *Celastrina ladon,* (Azure) (Figs. 1–2 after Verity; Figs. 3–5 after Scudder).

Fig. b. Patch of scales on wing of *Pieris napi* (after Verity).

Fig. c. Body of *Danaus plexippus* (Monarch).
I. Head. 1, antenna; 2, eye; 3, proboscis; 4, palpus; cl. clypeus; o, occiput.
II. Thorax. 5, prothoracic leg; 6, mesothoracic leg; 7, metathoracic leg; e, e, e, episterna; c, c, c, coxæ; tr., tr., trochanters of last two legs; f, f, femora of do.; s, s, s, scuta of first, second, and third segments of thorax.
III. Abdomen. 1–9 segments; sp., sp., spiracles (after Burgess).

Fig. d. Head and legs of *Œneis semidea,* showing aborted front leg.

Fig. e. Palpus of *Speyeria aphrodite* (Aphrodite Fritillary).

Fig. f. Leg of *Speyeria idalia* (Regal Fritillary). 1, coxa; 2, trochanter; 3, femur; 4, tibia; 5, tarsus.

Fig. g. Knobbed antenna of *Speyeria idalia.*

Fig. h. Clubbed antenna of *Limenitis astyanax* (Red-spotted Purple).

Fig. i. Hooked antenna of *Amblyscirtes vialis* (Common Roadside-Skipper).

and backward, upward and downward, as well as outward, all at one time.

In front, between the eyes and below the antennæ, are two little organs, each composed of three joints, which are known as the labial palpi (see Plate A, Fig. e). Between these, coiled up like a watch-spring, is the proboscis. This, when extended, acts rather like a drinking straw with which the butterfly sucks up nectar from flowers or drinks water from moist places (see Plate A, Figs. c and d).

The antennæ rise up between the eyes on the upper part of the head. The precise function of these organs in insects has been the subject of much discussion. Whether they function as ears, possess the sense of smell, combine these two senses, or represent a sense that is not present in vertebrates, their use in the life of insects is still not clearly understood. Evidence seems to be in favor of the view that they are organs of smell, and experiments have shown that the organs of hearing in insects are represented by certain pores and openings on their legs.

The thorax carries the organs of locomotion, which consist of four wings and six legs. It is made up of three segments or rings, the foremost of which is called the prothorax, the next the mesothorax, and the hindmost the metathorax. Because the bodies of butterflies are generally heavily clothed with hairs and scales, the subdivisions of the thorax are not easily distinguishable, even under a microscope, except by dissection.

The legs of butterflies are arranged in three pairs. The front pair known as prothoracic, being attached to the prothorax; the second pair called the mesothoracic, coming from the middle segment of the thorax; and the back pair, attached to the hindmost segment of the chest, referred to as the metathoracic legs. (see Plate A, Fig. c). It should be noted that in the family of the *Nymphalidæ*, or "Brushfooted Butterflies," in both sexes the front, or prothoracic pair of legs, are not fully developed (see Plate A, Fig. d), and therefore do not serve for walking. In the families of the *Riodinidæ*, or "Metalmarks," and the *Lycænidæ*, or "Blues and Coppers," the females have six legs adapted to walking, while the males possess only four ambulatory legs, the front pair being undeveloped, as they are in all the *Nymphalidæ*.

Like those of all other insects, the legs of butterflies consist of five parts (see Plate A, Fig. f). The first, nearest the body, is called the coxa, which articulates a small ring-like piece known as the trochanter. To the trochanter is attached the femur, and at an angle with the femur is the tibia. The last section of the leg is the tarsus, or foot, made up of a series of joints at the end of which is a pair of claws. In butterflies these are generally rather minute, though in other orders of insects the claws are sometimes long and powerful, as in some beetles.

In all *Nymphalidæ* and the males of the *Riodinidæ* and *Lycænidæ*, the prothoracic legs have lost the use of the tarsus except in feeble form, and the tibia has undergone modification. In many of the *Nymphalidæ* the tibia is densely clothed with long hairs, giving this part of the leg the appearance of a brush, from which comes the name "Brush-footed Butterflies" (see Plate A, Fig. d). The tibiæ are often armed with more or less strongly developed spines.

The wings are the most striking part of the butterfly which, in proportion to the size of its body, are usually very large and remarkable for the beauty of the colors and markings they display, both on the upper and on the undersides.

The wings are made up of a lacy network of horny double tubes, the inner filled with air, the outer one with blood. This blood is not red like the blood of vertebrates, but is almost colorless, or tinged with yellow. The circulation of blood in the outer wall of the wing-tubes takes place most freely during the brief time when the insect expands its wings after emergence from the chrysalis. When the butterfly has fully expanded its wings, the circulation of blood in the wings ceases almost entirely.

The horny tubes that compose the framework of butterfly wings support a delicate membrane, to both sides of which the scales are attached. The two forewings are more or less triangular in outline. The hindwings are generally subtriangular, more rounded on the outer margin, and in numerous forms have tail-like extentions.

Because in describing butterflies so much attention is devoted to the wing markings, it is important to be acquainted with the terms used for the different parts of the wings (see Plate B, Fig. 10). The part nearest to the thorax is called the base; the middle third of the wing is known as the median or discal area; and the outer third is the external or limbal area. The anterior margin of the wing is called the costal margin; the other edge is styled the external margin; the inner edge is known as the inner margin. The tip of the forewing—whether rounded, acute (pointed), falcate (sickle-shaped), or square—is called the apex (see Plate B, Figs. 1–4). The angle formed by the outer margin of the forewing with the inner margin is commonly known as the outer angle. The corresponding angle on the hindwing is known as the anal angle, and the point of the hindwing, corresponding with the tip or apex of the forewing, is designated the external angle. The margins of wings may have different outlines, and are spoken of as entire, crenulated, scalloped, waved, lobed, or tailed (see Plate B, Figs. 5–8).

A knowledge of the veins forming the framework of the wings is also important, because genera have frequently been established on the basis of wing structure. It is therefore useful to have some understanding of the nomenclature applied to the veins, although different writers having employed different terms to designate the same vein. Study the diagrams given on Plate B, Figs. 9 and 10. The veins in both the fore and hindwings of butterflies may be divided into simple and compound veins. In the forewing, the simple veins are the costal, the radials, the submedian, and the internal; in the hindwing they are the costal, the subcostal, the radials, the submedian, and the internal. The costal vein in the hind wing generally has, near the base, a short ascending branch known as the precostal vein.

In addition to the simple veins, the forewing has two branching veins, one immediately following the costal, known as the

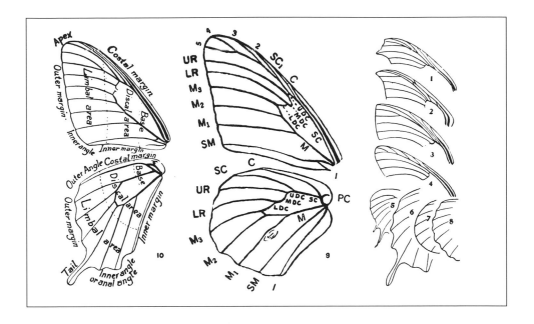

PLATE B

Fig. 1. *Angulated* or *acuminate apex* of forewing (*Polygonia-Anglewing*).

Fig. 2. *Falcate apex* of forewing (*Pyrrhanœa*).

Fig. 3. *Square apex* of forewing (*Smyrna*).

Fig. 4. *Rounded apex* of forewing (*Euptoieta*).

Fig. 5. Hindwing *rounded at outer angle, twice-tailed* (*Hairstreaks*).

Fig. 6. Hindwing *crenulate, tailed, lobed at anal angle* (*Papilio-Swallowtail*).

Fig. 7. Hindwing with *outer margin entire* (*Parnassius-Parnassian*).

Fig. 8. Hindwing with *outer margin waved* (*Speyeria*).

Fig. 9. Neuration of wings of *Danaus plexippus* (Monarch).

Veins: C, costal; SC, subcostal; M, median; SM, submedian; I, internal; PC, precostal; UDC, upper discocellular; MDC, middle discocellular; LDC, lower discocellular; UR, upper radial; LR, lower radial.

Nervules: SC 1, 2, 3, 4, 5, first to fifth subcostal nervules; M 1, 2, 3, first to third median nervules.

Fig. 10. Wing of *Papilio glaucus*, showing the names given to the different parts of the wings of butterflies.

subcostal, and the other preceding the sub-median, known as the median. The branches of these compound veins are known as nervules. The median vein always has three nervules. The nervules of the subcostal veins branch up and outward, with from four to five subcostal nervules, toward the costal margin and the apex of the forewing. In the hindwing, the subcostal vein is simple, but the median vein has three nervules, as in the forewing. Toward the base in both wings, between the subcostal and the median veins, lies the cell, which may be either enclosed or wholly or partially open at its outer extremity. The veinlets that close the cell are known as the discocellular veins. There are normally three, and branching from the point where they join are the radials, known respectively as upper and lower. In many genera, however, the upper radial can branch from the lower margin of the subcostal vein.

When at rest, butterflies generally hold their wings erect, the upper surfaces facing and only the undersides showing. In the genus *Hamadryas* the insect prefers, like some moths, to settle on the bark of trees with the wings spread flat and the head pointing downward. Many of the "Skippers," expand their hindwings horizontally when resting, while holding their forewings folded together, and "Hairstreaks," when resting on the end of a twig or leaf, will move their folded wings backward and forward, allowing the splendid blue surfaces of the upperside of their wings to be partially displayed first on one side and then on the other.

The abdomen of butterflies consists of nine segments (see Plate A, Fig. c). In most butterflies (except the *Ithomiids*) the end of the abdomen does not extend beyond the anal angle of the hindwings. A close examination of the abdomen of a butterfly reveals in each segment except the last a little valve-like orifice on either side. These openings are known as spiracles (see Plate A, Fig. c), and it is through these that the insect breathes. Insects do not breathe through their mouths, like vertebrates, and their lungs, or what correspond to the lungs of vertebrates, are not located in the thorax or chest, but in the abdomen.

The Nutritive System. Butterflies take their nourishment in fluid form, mostly as nectar from flowers. The proboscis, the organ of ingestion, communicates with the pharyngeal sac, a bulb-like receptacle in the head. It is controlled by a set of muscles that cause it to alternately expand and contract, much like a bulb-syringe. When the muscles expand, a vacuum is created and fluid is drawn up into the receptacle in the head; when they contract, a valve in front closes, a valve behind opens, and the honey in the receptacle is forced backward through the esophagus into the crop, and from there into the stomach.

The stomach lies on the ventral, or underside of the body but above the nervous cord. The stomach opens posteriorly into the small intestine, which is followed by the colon and, in turn, the rectum. Connected with the intestines are certain vesicles, the Malpighian vessels, which are believed to have a function similar to the liver of mammals.

The Circulatory and Respiratory Systems.
The heart of a butterfly, as in all arthropods, is located on the dorsal side of the body, a placement corresponding almost exactly to that of the spinal cord in vertebrate animals. It is a tubular organ with no ventricles and auricles, as in the heart of vertebrates, but with an enlargement in the mesothoracic region known as the aortal chamber.

The movement of the heart is wave-like, similar to the peristaltic movement of the intestines of vertebrates. Lateral blood vessels go out from the heart and intermingle with the capillary extremities of the tracheae, or bronchial tubes, which transport air from the spiracles. In this way, the blood is purified by oxygenation. The process takes place in the abdominal region, however, and not in the thorax, as with vertebrates.

The Nervous System. In butterflies, the nervous system consists of a cord with nerve-knots, or ganglia, one for each segment of the body. As there are thirteen segments in the body of a butterfly, there are normally thirteen ganglia, or nerve centers. The nervous cord lies in a position exactly opposite that of the spinal cord in vertebrates. It is situated on the ventral side, closer to the underside of the body than all the other internal organs.

The ganglion in the head is the largest of all and forms a rudimentary brain, the greater portion of which consists of two relatively large optic nerves.

The Reproductive System. The external organs of generation are found at the end of the abdomen of a butterfly. The male may be distinguished from the female by two flattish, scale-like appendages or "claspers," called pre-hensores, which adhere one on either side to the last segment of the body. These organs are quite peculiar in their structure, and it is possible by means of them to distinguish closely allied species, especially among the *Hesperiidæ* (Skippers). The abdomen of the female does not have claspers, and is generally plumper, especially when the eggs have not yet been deposited.

The internal organs of reproduction in the female consist of ovaries. Eggs pass from the ovaries into the oviduct and from there to the ovipositor. Communicating with the oviduct are spermatothecæ, or receptacles that retain the fertilizing fluid received from the male during mating. As the eggs pass through the oviduct they are impregnated by the spermatozoa, which enter their walls.

The internal organs of reproduction in the male are tubular vesicles, or testes. They secrete seminal fluid by means of an organ that is introduced into the spermatothecæ of the female. Generally, union between the sexes takes place once and is not recurrent. Once the female has been impregnated, she proceeds at once to lay her eggs on tender leaves, flower buds, or the bark of plants that will nourish her young, after which she dies. For a butterfly, life in the winged form is usually very brief.

To find a pair of mating insects can be the only way to settle definitely the question of male and female within forms. Some are so different that the two sexes were described by early writers as belonging not merely to different species, but to different genera, and even families.

THE LIFE HISTORY OF BUTTERFLIES

Butterflies undergo great changes, or metamorphoses, during their brief lives, as do almost all insects. They exist first as eggs; then they appear as caterpillars; the third stage is that of the chrysalis; the final stage is that of the imago, or fully-developed adult insect.

The Eggs of Butterflies

The eggs of butterflies are beautiful objects when examined under a glass. Various in form, some are spheres or half spheres, some are conical, cylindrical or spindle-shaped, others are flat and resemble little cheeses, and still others are turban shaped. The egg surfaces may be smooth, adorned with raised ribs and sculpturings (see Plate C, Figs. f and g) or marked with little depressions or pitting arranged in geometrical patterns. Some are white, some pale green, or blue-green; others are yellow, orange, red, or purple. They are often spotted and marbled like the eggs of some birds.

Eggs are deposited by the female on the plants appropriate to the development of the larvae. Most species are restricted to certain species or genera of plants. Caterpillars are rarely promiscuous feeders, and even when a species is known to eat different plants, it has been observed that one caterpillar, having begun to feed upon a certain plant, will prefer this to all others, and will not willingly accept anything else. For instance, larvae that feed in nature on either wild plum or lilac, if they begin to feed on one will steadily refuse the other if it is offered to them. A fascinating thing in nature is the way a female butterfly invariably selects the plant that will best meet the needs of progeny she never lives to see.

The eggs are deposited sometimes singly, sometimes in small clusters, sometimes in a mass. Fertile eggs undergo a change in color soon after they have been laid. It is possible at this point to see through the thin shell with a magnifying glass, and view the form of the caterpillar that is developing inside.

When the development is completed the caterpillar emerges from an opening at either the side or top of the egg. Many species have eggs with a sort of lid, a portion of the shell being separated by a thin section that breaks under the pressure of the enlarging embryo. This portion flies off, while the rest adheres to the twig or leaf to which it was attached. Many larvæ, as soon as they have emerged from the egg, make their first meal of the shell from which they have just escaped.

Caterpillars

The second stage is known as the larval stage. When it is reached the insect is spoken of as a larva, or caterpillar (see Plate C, Fig. h). Caterpillars have long, worm-like bodies, often thickest about the middle, tapering at each end, and more or less flat on the underside. Sometimes caterpillars are oval or slug-shaped. Frequently, their bodies are adorned with hairs, spines, and tubercles of various forms. The body of the larva, like the body of the butterfly, consists normally of thirteen rings or segments, of which the three just behind the head correspond to the prothorax, the mesothorax, and the metathorax of the butterfly, while the remaining nine correspond to its abdomen.

The three front segments have legs that correspond in location to the legs of the winged form, and are known as the true legs of the larva. Besides these, the caterpillar has, at about mid-body and at its posterior end, paired pro-legs, as they are called. These are its principal organs of locomotion in this stage, but do not reappear in the butterfly.

The mouth parts of caterpillars are profoundly different from those of the butterfly. The imago lives on fluid nourishment, and is provided with the proboscis, a sucking organ. The caterpillar, on the other hand, is armed with a pair of cutting mandibles, with which it shears off tiny strips of the leaves upon which it feeds. It holds the edge of the leaf in place with the three pairs of true legs, while it supports its body on the pro-legs during the act of eating.

In many cases, the caterpillar's head is very large in proportion to the rest of the body when it first emerges from the egg, but as growth takes place, this disparity disappears. As the larva grows, it soon reaches a point when its skin becomes too small and tight. It then proceeds to moult, or shed. First, the caterpillar anchors this outer skin by strands of silk to the leaf or branch upon which the moult is to take place. The skin then splits along the back and the caterpillar crawls out. Having escaped from the cast-off garment, the caterpillar sometimes turns around and eats it before resuming its vegetable diet. The process of moulting takes place four or five times before the larva changes into a chrysalis. Each period between moults is known as an instar.

Caterpillars differ from butterflies in that they are able to produce silk. Silk is a viscous fluid secreted by elongated sacs located in the dorsal region. These sacs communicate with a minute tube-like organ, known as the spinneret, which is located on the underside of the head of the caterpillar, just behind the mandibles. The fluid silk, ejected through the spinneret, immediately hardens on contact with the air and becomes very fine threads or filaments that the caterpillar uses for various purposes. It may form a line with which to guide itself from place to place and enable it to retrace its steps to a favorite resting-place, or tie together leaves as a nest, or weave a sort of shelter in which to conceal itself. Finally it uses silk to make little buttons and harnesses by which, as we shall see later, the chrysalis is held in place. Many moths weave cocoons, in which the chrysalis is lodged, but butterflies do not weave true cocoons.

Time spent in the egg is generally short. The time passed in the larval state may be short or long. When butterflies hibernate as caterpillars, time spent in this state is long—especially for those species in arctic regions where warm seasons are short. Some butterflies north of the Arctic Circle, because the summers are so short in the far north, pass two summers and the intervening winter in the larval condition, and then another winter in the pupal stage, before they emerge and take wing. On the other hand, under more temperate conditions, butterflies of certain species may produce two or even three broods in a summer, and in subtropical or tropical lands there may be even more broods produced.

Almost all larvæ of *Lepidoptera* subsist on vegetable food, but there are exceptions. One such is the Harvester, *Feniseca tarquinius* (see pages 120–121), whose slug-like larva feeds on scale-insects, or mealy bugs, sharing this trait with certain allied species in Africa and Asia.

The Pupa, or Chrysalis

The third stage in the life of *Lepidoptera* is known as the pupal stage. The caterpillar, after successive moults, is transformed into a pupa, or chrysalis (see Plate C, Figs. d and e). From being an active, worm-like creature, greedily feeding upon its appropriate food, it reverts to a form that is stationary, as was the egg, and ceases to have the power of locomotion.

A chrysalid contains an immature butterfly. Segments of the chrysalid enclose corresponding segments of the butterfly, and the wings and all other organs are enfolded in sheathing plates of chitinous, or horn-like, matter. The transformation from the caterpillar stage to the pupal stage is very wonderful. The caterpillar makes provision for the change by weaving a little button of silk and, in cases where the chrysalid will not just hang, by also weaving a harness of silk, which it passes around its back, and that holds it in place very much as lines of tackle support a climber (see Plate C, Fig. e). The caterpillar now becomes very quiet, its hind pro-legs being securely entangled and hooked into the silken button. When the proper moment has arrived, the skin of the caterpillar splits, just as in earlier moults, and by a series of wriggling or vibratory motions the chrysalis works off the skin of the caterpillar until it has all been shed except where, near the end of the abdomen, the skin is caught between two of the horny rings which form the abdomen. The insect then feels around with its cremaster, a little spikelet armed with small hooks at the very tip of the chrysalis, until these hooks become entangled in the silk of the button that had been deposited on the under surface of a twig, a stone, or a fence rail, where the transformation is occurring. As soon as the chrysalis is securely hooked into the button of silk, it lets go of the little section of skin by which it has been supported and rapidly assumes the shape in which it will remain until the time of its emergence as a butterfly. These changes are illustrated on Plate C, Figs. a–d.

The chrysalids of all the *Nymphalidæ* (Brushfoots) are pendant; those of the other families, except the *Hesperiidæ* (Skippers), use harnesses, as shown on Plate C, in the figures representing the chrysalis of *Battus philenor* (Pipevine Swallowtail). The *Hesperiidæ* chrysalids, like the chrysalids of moths, are either formed in loosely woven coverings of leaves tacked together with silken threads, or lie free under dried leaves and other decaying plants on the ground.

Chrysalids are for the most part rather obscure in coloring, though some are quite brilliantly marked with metallic spots. The chrysalis of the common *Danaus plexippus* (Monarch), is pearly green, ornamented with bright golden spots.

The forms assumed by chrysalids are varied, especially among the *Nymphalidæ*, and they are often ornamented with curious projections and tubercles, giving them very odd outlines.

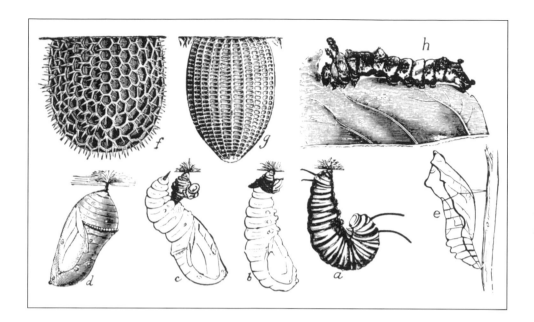

PLATE C

Caterpillar of *Danaus plexippus* (Monarch):

Fig. a. Ready to change into a chrysalis;

Fig. b. Having partly shed its skin;

Fig. c. Holding itself suspended by grasping the shed skin between the edges of the third and fourth abdominal segments; feeling with the cremaster for the button of silk above;

Fig. d. Having caught the button and assumed its final form as a chrysalis.

Fig. e. Chrysalis of *Battus philenor* (Pipevine Swallowtail), held by button and girdle of silk.

Fig. f. Egg of *Limenitis archippus* (Viceroy), greatly magnified.

Fig. g. Egg of *Danaus plexippus* (Monarch), greatly magnified.

Fig. h. Caterpillar of *Limenitis archippus* (Viceroy).

Some butterflies remain in the chrysalis stage for only a few days or weeks; others pass the winter in this state, as is true of many of the species found in the colder parts of North America. In temperate regions, some butterflies have as many as three broods: the spring brood, coming from chrysalids that have over-wintered, an early summer brood, and a fall brood. In tropical countries many species retain the form of the chrysalis during the dry season, and emerge at the beginning of the rainy season, when vegetation is refreshed and new and tender growth takes place in the forests.

The Imago, or Winged Insect

How the butterfly undergoes transformation from the chrysalis is every bit as interesting as when the caterpillar changes into the pupa.

First, the sheath covering the head, legs, and antennæ splits, the head protrudes, and the forelegs are disentangled and pushed out. They are followed almost at once by the other legs, and the insect then crawls out of the pupal skin, emerging with the wings as miniature objects, the body trailing after as a long worm-like mass. The insect immediately assumes a stationary position, head upward, body hanging downward. The action of the heart rapidly sends the fluids in the body into circulation, particularly into the wings, which expand minute by minute, the fluids being transferred through the network of the wings until they have assumed their full form.

The insect begins to gently fan its wings while remaining in the same position. After the wings become perfectly dry, and the long, worm-like body shrinks up to assume the form it will retain through the subsequent life of the insect, the butterfly begins to change position, carefully crawling a few steps to try out its powers of locomotion. It expands its wings, and, presto! it is fluttering off in quest of food.

KEY TO THE SUBFAMILIES OF THE NYMPHALIDÆ OF TEMPERATE NORTH AMERICA

I. With the veins of the forewings not greatly swollen at the base.
    A. Antennæ naked, not clothed with scales.
        (a) Forewings less than twice as long as broad. *Euplœinæ*
        (b) Forewings twice as long as broad and often translucent, the abdomen extending far beyond the inner angle of the hindwings. *Ithomiinæ*
    B. Antennæ clothed with scales, at least above.
        (a) Forewings at least twice as long as broad. *Heliconiinæ*
        (b) Forewings less than twice as long as broad.
            1. Palpi not as long as the thorax. *Nymphalinæ*
            2. Palpi longer than the thorax. *Libytheinæ*
II. With some of the veins of the forewing greatly swollen at the base. *Satyrinæ*

CLASSIFICATION OF BUTTERFLIES

▶ Class INSECTA (Insects)
▶ Order LEPIDOPTERA (Scale-winged Insects)
▶ Sub-order RHOPALOCERA (Butterflies)

The classification of the genera and species of butterflies is broken down further into families. Represented in the United States and Canada are these six families of butterflies:

"Brushfooted Butterflies" *Nymphalidæ*

"Metalmarks" *Riodinidæ*

"Blues," "Coppers," "Hairstreaks" *Lycænidæ*

"Swallowtails," and their allies *Papilionidæ*

"Skippers" *Hesperiidæ*

"Whites" and "Sulphurs" *Pieridæ*

Family NYMPHALIDÆ (The Brushfooted Butterflies)

The *Nymphalidæ* may be distinguished from all other butterflies by the fact that in both sexes the prothoracic or foremost pair of legs is dwarfed, useless for walking, and carried folded up against the breast. This is the largest of all the families of butterflies and it has been subdivided into many subfamilies. Some of the genera have small species, but most of them are made up of medium-sized or large butterflies. Many of the most gorgeously colored butterflies of the tropics belong to this family, among them the brilliant blue Morphos of equatorial America.

The caterpillars, when they emerge from the egg, have heads much greater in diameter than the rest of their bodies. In the earlier stages the bodies taper backward and have little wart-like protuberances with hairs. In later stages these little protuberances, in many genera are replaced by branching spines and fleshy projections, giving the caterpillars a forbidding appearance. The mature caterpillar generally has a cylindrical body, but in the Satyrs and Morphos, the larvæ are thicker at the middle, tapering forward and backward.

The chrysalids, generally marked by metallic spots, always hang suspended by the tail, except in the case of a few arctic species. These are found under a frail covering made from strands of silk woven around the roots of grass tufts, where the larva takes shelter at the time of pupation.

In the region covered by this book, all the butterflies belonging to the *Nymphalidæ* fall into one of the following subfamilies:

(1) the Euplœids *Euplœinæ*
(2) the Ithomiids *Ithomiinæ*
(3) the Heliconians *Heliconiinæ*
(4) the Nymphs *Nymphalinæ*
(5) the Satyrs *Satyrinæ*
(6) the Snout-butterflies *Libytheinæ*

Subfamily EUPLŒINÆ (now Danainae, The Monarchs)

These butterflies are large or medium-sized with forewings somewhat elongated at the apex. The hindwings are rounded, never with tails, those of the males marked with one or more sexual brands, which in the American species are located on or near the first median nervule. The forelegs are greatly atrophied in the males, somewhat less so in the females.

All of the American species are of some shade of reddish-brown or tan, with the apex of the forewings and the outer borders of both fore- and hindwings margined widely with darker color, the veins and nervules also darker, standing out in bold relief on the lighter ground-color. The apex of the primary and the outer border of the secondary wings are more or less spotted with light color, often with white.

The adult caterpillars are cylindrical in form, of some light shade of yellow or green banded with darker colors, and adorned with long fleshy filaments. The American species feeds upon the plants belonging to the family of the *Asclepiadaceæ*, or Milkweeds. The chrysalis is smooth, pale in color, often ornamented with metallic spots, usually golden.

This subfamily, which is represented in the tropics of the Old World by many genera and species, is only represented in the United States by one genus, *Danaus*.

Subfamily ITHOMIINÆ (The Ithomiids, Clearwings)

The butterflies in this subfamily are of moderate size, though a few species are quite large. The wings are more or less transparent, the forewings at least twice as long as wide, and the hindwings small, rounded, and without tails. The abdomen projects beyond the margin of the hindwing. The antennæ are long, naked, and very thin, with a slender club at the end. The forelegs are greatly atrophied, especially in the males.

The larvæ and chrysalids resemble those of the *Danainæ* (Monarchs), the chrysalids being short, cylindrical, and marked with metallic spots. The family is mostly confined to the Americas. There are swarms of genera and species in the South American tropics. Like the *Danainæ* (Monarchs) they are "pro-tected." Two genera are reported from our territory.

Subfamily HELICONIINÆ (The Heliconians)

Heliconians are moderately large butterflies with forewings twice as long as wide. Their color is mostly black, sometimes shot with blue, and variously marked with white, yellow, orange, or crimson spots.

Their antennæ are nearly as long as their bodies, with a tapering club, stouter than in the Ithomiids, and covered with scales above. The forelegs are feeble in both sexes. The eggs are cylindrical, ribbed, twice as high as wide, tapering and truncate above. The caterpillar, when mature, has six branching spines on each segment. Its chrysalis is angulate, dark in color and covered with curious projections, making it look like a shrivelled leaf.

These insects are strongly "protected," and found in the forests of tropical America. There are many species, but only one occurs in our region.

Subfamily NYMPHALINÆ (The Nymphs)

The butterflies belonging to this subfamily are usually medium-sized or large, although some are very small. The antennæ are usually as long as, or longer than, the abdomen, and more or less heavily clothed with scales. Its palpi are stout, densely clothed with hairs and scales. They have a very robust thorax. The forewings are relatively broad, except in certain forms that mimic the *Heliconiinæ*, and elongated at the apex, having a more or less excavated outer margin. The discoidal cell is generally less than half the length of wing, often open, or closed by an almost imperceptible veinlet. The costal vein ends behind the middle of the front margin of the wing, and the two inner subcostal nervules branch off before, the outer subcostals beyond, the end of the cell. The hindwings can be rounded or angulate, with the outer border either rounded, scalloped, or tailed. The inner border always forms a channel for the abdomen.

The eggs are conoid, barrel-shaped or globular, and variously ornamented. The larva is covered with tiny, wart-like nubs when hatched, each with a hair, the hairs in later stages replaced in many forms by branching spines. The chrysalis hangs suspended, and is variously ornamented, often having raised points down the back and a two-lobed head.

In the United States, there are about thirty genera, containing somewhat less than two hundred species, belonging to this subfamily.

Subfamily LIBYTHEINÆ (The Snout-butterflies or Snouts)

These insects can be distinguished from all others by their long projecting palpi, and by the fact that the males have only four feet adapted to walking while the females have six, a fact which seems to ally them to the *Erycinidæ*. On the other hand, the chrysalis is pendent as in the *Nymphalidæ*. There is only one genus of the group represented in our faunal region.

Subfamily SATYRINÆ (The Satyrs)

The butterflies in this subfamily are generally of medium size, obscure in color, their wings, especially on the underside, ornamented with dark eye-like spots, pupilled in the centre with a light point and ringed around with one or more circles of lighter color. They have a weak flight, dancing about in the vegetation and often hiding among grasses and weeds. Most of them are forest-loving, but some live on the summits of bleak and cold mountains, others on the verge of arctic snows, and some on the prairies.

The veins of the forewings are generally greatly swollen at the base, thus enabling them to be distinguished from almost all other butterflies. The eggs are subspherical, somewhat higher than broad, ribbed on the sides, particularly at the apex, and rounded at the base. Caterpillars, when they emerge from the egg, have heads much bigger in diameter than the rest of the body, but as they mature they lose this feature, and generally taper from the middle of the body in either direction. Anal pro-legs bifurcating, thus readily distinguished from all other caterpillars, except those of the genus *Chlorippe*. They feed on grasses and sedges, concealing themselves in the daytime and coming out to feed at night. The chrysalids are short and stout, plain both in color and outline.

There are about sixty species of Satyrs in this region, but only a few examples are represented here.

Family RIODINIDÆ (formerly, ERYCINDÆ) (The Metalmarks)

This is a large family of small or rather less than medium-sized butterflies, which is found in both the eastern and western hemispheres, but is mostly confined to the

American tropics, where there are known to be about a thousand species, some of them remarkably beautiful in their colors and markings. The males have the forelegs aborted as in the case of the *Nymphalidæ*, while the females have six legs for walking. In this respect they resemble the *Lycænidæ*. The chrysalids are not pendant as are those of all the insects which we have hitherto described in this book, but are held in place by a silken girdle, and are closely appressed to the supporting surface. The strongest mark of distinction from other butterflies is the fact that the precostal vein of the hindwing is located on the extreme inner margin of the wing and sends out a little free hook, very much as is the case in many of the moths. The antennæ are very long and slender, distinctly knobbed at the end. Many genera have the peculiarity when alighting of not folding their wings, but carrying them flat, and they have also the habit of hiding under leaves, like moths. Most of the species found in our region occur in the Southwestern States, two alone are found in the Eastern States.

Family LYCÆNIDÆ (The Hair-streaks, Coppers, and Blues)

Small butterflies. The males have the first pair of legs more or less aborted, and not adapted to walking. Many of the genera are brilliantly blue on the upperside of the wings, others are coppery red. In Africa there are numerous genera which mimic other butterflies in the form and color of their wings. The eggs are turban-shaped adorned with ridges, minute eminences, and networks of raised lines. Under the microscope some of them look like sea-urchins after the spines have fallen off. The caterpillars are slug-shaped, flat; and while most of them feed on vegetable matter a few feed on scale-insects and aphids, and some on the larvæ of ants. The latter are African and Oriental forms. The chrysalids are attached to the place where the caterpillar has pupated by a cincture or girdle.

The family is very large and is represented in all parts of the world, but there are probably more species in the American tropics than in any other quarter of the globe, unless it be in the Malaysian Archipelago and New Guinea, from which a host of species have been described in recent years.

A multitude of refinements in classification have been invented by recent authors and a lot of generic names have been proposed which in this book we shall in part ignore, as they are based upon such slight points that nobody but a man armed with a big microscope can make them out. They puzzle common people, and this book is for laymen and not for the supertechnical.

Family PAPILIONIDÆ (The Swallowtails and Allies)

The butterflies of this group are provided in both sexes with six legs adapted to walking. The internal vein of the hindwing is wanting, its place being taken by the submedian. The caterpillars are elongate, and in the genus *Papilio* provided with osmeteria or protrusive forking scent-organs, which, when the caterpillar is disturbed, they thrust forth from the pouch back of the head in which they usually lie concealed. Chrysalids in all the genera are more or less elongate, attached at the anal extremity to a button of silk, and held in place by a silk girdle, but never closely appressed to the supporting surface as is the case in the *Erycinidæ* and *Lycænidæ*.

Subfamily PIERINÆ (The Yellows, Sulphurs, and Whites)

For the most part small or medium-sized butterflies, white or yellow in color, with dark marginal markings. The eggs are spindle-shaped, marked with vertical ridges and horizontal cross-lines. The caterpillars are cylindrical, relatively long, generally green in color, with longitudinal stripes. The chrysalids are more or less pointed at the head, with the wingcases greatly developed on the ventral lower side, forming a more or less keel-shaped projection upon this surface.

The subfamily is very large, and is well represented in the tropics of both the eastern and western hemispheres. Certain genera are also widely distributed in the colder regions of both the north and the south, among them the genus *Colias*, species of which occur from Greenland to Patagonia and from the North Cape to the Cape of Good Hope.

Subfamily PARNASSIINÆ (The Parnassians)

This peculiar group of butterflies is classed with the *Papilionidæ* (Swallowtails) because the internal vein of the hindwings is always lacking, a characteristic of all *papilionine* genera. The caterpillars are not provided with osmeteria, or offensive scent-organs, and pupation takes place upon the ground among loosely scattered leaves which are interwoven by the larva with a few loose strands of silk. The insects are mainly inhabitants of the mountain regions of the northern hemisphere.

Subfamily PAPILIONINÆ (The Swallowtails)

Large butterflies. As shown on Plate A, Fig. 10, the hindwings lack the internal vein, its place being held by the submedian vein. There is great diversity of form in this group. Many species are tailed, as are the three occurring in Europe, and the name, common in England, has come in popular phrase to be loosely applied to the whole genus.

There are many hundreds of species and varietal forms, most of which occur in the tropics of the eastern and western hemispheres. There are only three species found in all Europe; there are about thirty found in the United States and Canada.

Family HESPERIIDÆ (The Skippers)

Generally quite small butterflies, with a stout thorax. Both sexes have six feet adapted to walking. The tibiæ of the hind legs, with few exceptions, have spurs. The lower radial vein of the hindwing in many genera is lacking, being represented by a fold in the wing. The eggs are hemispherical, flat on base. The larvæ are cylindrical, tapering from the middle before and behind, with large globular heads, smooth. The chrysalids are generally formed on the ground or among leaves and litter lightly tacked together with a few strands of silk, in which the cremaster is caught.

A large family, most numerously represented in the tropics of both the Old and

New Worlds. About three thousand species are known, of which over one hundred occur within our limits.

Subfamily PYRRHOPYGINÆ
(The Red-tailed Skippers or Firetips)

Rather large butterflies when compared with others in the family. The antennæ terminate in a long, thick, blunt club, forming a regular curve, looking in outline like the handle of an old-fashioned walkingstick. Most of the species are red at the end of the abdomen. Confined to the New World. Only one genus and species of this family occurs within our borders.

Subfamily PYRGINÆ
(The Hesperids or Spread-wing Skippers)

The forewing is generally provided with a costal fold, but never marked with a sexual brand or raised patch of scales on the disc. The hindwing may be provided with a lengthy tail or simply lobed at the anal angle. The antennæ terminate in a fine point, which in some genera is bent backward at right angles to the shaft.

Subfamily PAMPHILINÆ
(The Pamphilids or Grass-Skippers)

The male never has a costal fold on the forewing, but in most of the genera has a discal stigma on the forewing, the only exceptions to this in our fauna being in the case of the three genera *Amblyscirtes* (Roadside

Skippers), *Carterocephalos* (Arctic Skippers), and *Oarisma* (Skipperlings). The antennæ are short, in some genera very short, clubbed at the end and provided in many genera with a little finely pointed tip at the end of the club, which sometimes is bent backward. The third joint of the palpi is generally small, inconspicuous, and often pointing forward. The lower radial vein in the forewing always is nearer to the median than to the upper radial; the lower radial in the hindwing is generally lacking. When at rest they raise the forewings, folding them together, while the hindwings are held horizontally. This attitude is characteristic of this subfamily, giving rise to one of their modern names, "Folded-wing Skippers."

Subfamily MEGATHYMINÆ
(The Giant-Skippers)

These curious insects have been by some writers placed among the *Castniidæ*, a family of day-flying moths, but as the author stated in 1898 in "The Butterfly Book," they appear to have much more in common with the *Hesperiidæ* than the *Castniidæ*. The proposition to include them in the *Hesperiidæ* as a subfamily under the name given above has since that time been generally accepted by systematists. There are a number of species belonging to the genus *Megathymus*, several of which occur within our faunal limits.

To review the current classification now in use by NABA, The North American Butterfly Association, Inc.., see page 209.

THE SPECIES

Danaus (formerly Anosia)
Genus

These are large or medium-sized butterflies, with triangular forewings that are somewhat elongated. The hindwings are rounded, with inner margins of the wings that clasp the butterfly's abdomen when it is at rest. The apex, outer margins, and veins of the wings are dark. The male has a sex-mark on the first median nervule of the hindwing.

The eggs are rounded cones, ribbed both perpendicularly and horizontally. The larva is cylindrical, with long, dark, fleshy filaments in front and back. The larva is usually pale in color and ringed with dark bands. The chrysalis is also pale with metallic spots and an abdomen rapidly tapering and ending in a long cremaster. It is cylindrical, stout, and pendant, anchored only at one end.

This is a large genus, with many species in the tropics of both hemispheres, but only three in the United States. The insects are "protected" by their brilliant coloring, which signals to predators that they are distasteful, because of the poisons in the milkweed plants that their caterpillars eat.

Danaus plexippus
▸ **Monarch**

The upperside of the Monarch's wings are orange or reddish-brown. The apex, margins, and veins are black. The undersides of the wings are paler. On the outer borders of the wings there is a double row of whitish spots, and the apex is also crossed by two bands of light spots. Wing expanse is 3.25 to 4.25 inches. Monarch eggs are pale green, and its caterpillar feeds on milkweeds. The chrysalis is pale green spotted with gold. (See Plate C, page 17): Fig. g, egg; Figs. a–c, larva pupating; Fig. d, chrysalis.)

This species has several broods each year. As summer comes, the butterflies move north, laying eggs. They spread up into their northern limit in Canada. In fall they return. Swarms of the retreating butterflies gather on the northern shores of Lakes Erie and Ontario and in southern New Jersey on their way southward to their wintering sites in Central America.

Danaus gilippus
▸ **Queen**

The markings of this butterfly are somewhat different from those of the preceding species. This species is smaller than the Monarch, and the ground-color of the wings is a reddish-brown. The wing expanse is 2.5 to 3 inches. The Queen is not found in the North, but ranges through New Mexico, Texas, Arizona, and southward.

Editor's note: In 1975, long after Holland's time, the Monarchs' wintering sites were discovered in the mountains of Mexico.

Above right: *Monarchs on goldenrod.*
Below right: *Queen nectaring on a daisy.*

COMMON NAME	Monarch
FAMILY	Brushfooted Butterflies
GROUP	Milkweed Butterflies
COMMON NAME	Queen
FAMILY	Brushfooted Butterflies
GROUP	Milkweed Butterflies

Heliconius
Genus

Above: *Zebra Longwings.*

The Longwings. These are moderately large butterflies. Their forewings are twice as long as they are wide. The butterfly's antennæ are nearly as long as the body, with a tapering club that has scales along the top. The forelegs are feeble in both sexes. The predominant color is black, sometimes shot with blue, and variously marked with white, yellow, orange, or crimson spots.

The eggs are cylindrical, ribbed, twice as long as wide, tapered but blunt on top. The mature caterpillar has six branching spines on each segment of its body. The chrysalids are dark in color, angular and covered with curious projections, making them look like shrivelled leaves. These insects, which are strongly "protected" by their markings and colors, abound in the forests of tropical America. There are many species, but only one occurs in our region.

Heliconius charithonia
▸ Zebra Heliconian

The caterpillar feeds upon the foliage of different species of *Passiflora*. The Zebra's wing expanse is 2.5 to 3.5 inches. The Zebra butterfly is common in hot parts of the Gulf States, ranging from there all over the American tropics.

COMMON NAME Zebra Heliconian

FAMILY Brushfooted Butterflies

GROUP Longwings

Dryas
Genus

Above: *Julia Longwing.*

The butterflies of this genus mimic the Heliconians in form. Their forewings are long and narrow and the cell in the hindwing is open. There are a number of species, two of which are found in the hot parts of the Gulf States. The larvæ resemble those of the genera, *Agraulis* and *Euptoieta*, being reddish-brown with black hairs, and, like them, they feed on *Passiflora*.

Dryas iulia
▶ Julia Heliconian

This insect occurs sparingly in Florida and in Texas, especially around Brownsville. It is very common in Mexico and south of there. The wing expanse is 3 to 3.5 inches.

COMMON NAME Julia Heliconian

FAMILY Brushfooted Butterflies

GROUP Longwings

Agraulis
Genus

This genus has elongated forewings, but less so than in *Dryas*. The cell in the hindwing is open. The palpi are much more robust and heavily clothed with hairs than in *Dryas*, thus resembling those of the genus *Speyeria*. Like *Speyeria*, the undersides of the wings of all species of *Agraulis* are spotted with silver.

There are a half dozen species of *Agraulis* in the Americas, but only one occurs within the regions we are covering. They are gloriously beautiful insects.

Agraulis vanillæ
▸ **Gulf Fritillary**

This lovely insect ranges from southern Virginia southward and westward to southern California, and from there even further south—wherever the sun shines and *Passiflora* blooms. The wing expanse of this Fritillary is 2.75 to 3.25 inches.

Above: *Gulf Fritillary—underside showing silver spots.* **Above right:** *Gulf Fritillary.* **Below right:** *Larva of Gulf Fritillary on host plant (passionflower).*

COMMON NAME Gulf Fritillary

FAMILY Brushfooted Butterflies

GROUP Fritillaries

Two species of this genus are found in the United States. The butterfly has the cell of the forewing closed by a feeble veinlet and the cell of the hindwing open. The antennæ and palpi resemble those of the genus *Speyeria*. The undersides of the wings are not spotted with silvery marks.

Euptoieta claudia
▸ Variegated Fritillary

The caterpillar feeds upon the leaves of passion flowers and violets. It is reddish-yellow in color, with black spines on the segments, white spots on the back, and dark brown bands running the long way on the sides. The chrysalis is pearly white-mottled with black spots and streaks. The insect ranges from southern New England south and west, and is reported from as far north as Alberta. It goes as far as Argentina in the south. Wing expanse – male: 1.75 to 2.25 inches; female: 2.25 to 2.75 inches.

Above: *Variegated Fritillary sipping nectar from a flower.*
Right: *Variegated Fritillary.*

Euptoieta hegesia
▸ Mexican Fritillary

Very much like the preceding species, only the wings, especially the hindwings, have very few dark markings, except around the borders, making it look golden in color, and the insect is smaller. The wing expanse in the male is 1.6 to 2.25 inches, in the female, 2.25 to 2.5 inches. This butterfly is found in Texas, Arizona, and south into Mexico.

COMMON NAME Variegated Fritillary
FAMILY Brushfooted Butterflies
GROUP Fritillaries

COMMON NAME Mexican Fritillary
FAMILY Brushfooted Butterflies
GROUP Fritillaries

Speyeria (formerly Argynnis)

These butterflies are of medium or large size, generally of some shade of reddish-tan, conspicuously marked on the upperside with dark spots and waved lines, which are less conspicuously repeated on the underside, and in many species in part replaced by silvery spots. In some species the males and the females are dimorphic, that is, very different in appearance from each other. The palpi are strongly developed and clothed heavily with hairs. The antennæ have a short, well-defined, flattened, somewhat spoon-shaped club. The cells of both fore- and hindwings are closed. Eggs are cone-shaped, flattened, and depressed at the top, rounded at the base, ribbed both ways, mostly near the base. The caterpillars are dark in color, spiny, with the spines on the first segment the longest. They feed on violets at night and hide during the day. The chrysalis is angular, adorned with more or less prominent projections; the head is bifid or two-lobed.

This large genus has many species, occurring in both hemispheres, but its metropolis is North America. A few examples of the more conspicuous forms are represented here.

Speyeria cybele
▸ Great Spangled Fritillary

The male is bright reddish-tan on the upper side of the wings, with the characteristic dark markings of the genus. The underside of the wings are heavily silvered. There is always a pale yellowish submarginal band shown on the underside of the hind wings which does not appear in the next species, S. *aphrodite*, and it is by the presence or absence of this that one can tell them apart. The caterpillars hibernate as soon as they are hatched, and pass the winter in this state, feeding up and maturing in the following spring when the violets begin to grow. The wing expanse is 3 to 4 inches.

This species ranges from Maine to Nebraska and southward to Georgia and Arkansas. It is our commonest species in the Middle States.

Above right: *Great Spangled Fritillary nectaring on a zinnia flower.* **Below right:** *Great Spangled Fritillary feeding at a butterflyweed (Asclepias tuberosa).*

COMMON NAME Great Spangled Fritillary

FAMILY Brushfooted Butterflies

GROUP Fritillary

Speyeria (formerly Argynnis)
Genus

It should be remarked that genus *Speyeria* is very difficult. It is similar to the genus *Salix*, the willows, among plants. Botanists know how the willows seem to run together, and how hard it is to discriminate between the species. The same thing is true of this great genus of butterflies. It is particularly true of the species occurring in the region of the Rocky Mountains. The test of breeding has not been fully applied to all of these forms, and it is doubtful whether some of them are more than varieties or local races. This is a field of inquiry to tempt some ardent student. Entomological study would benefit from being more intensive, as well as extensive.

Speyeria aphrodite
▸ Aphrodite Fritillary

This butterfly closely resembles the preceding species, but it is slightly smaller. The submarginal band is narrower on the underside of the hindwings than in *S. cybele* and is often completely missing. The underside of the forewings is redder at the base than in *S. cybele*. The wing expanse is 3 to 3.5 inches. The range is the same as for *S. cybele*, being from Maine to Nebraska and southward to Georgia and Arkansas.

The two species *S. cybele* and *S. aphrodite* usually are found flying at the same time and in the same places, and when on the wing it is often very difficult to distinguish them from each other. In fact they seem to intergrade into each other, and in a long series of specimens, such close resemblances often occur that it is puzzling to decide which is which. The deeper red of the forewing of *S. cybele* is the best diacritical character. The paler outer margin of the hindwing of *S. Aphrodite* sometimes occurs also in *S. cybele*.

Above right: *Aphrodite Fritillary nectaring on thistle.*
Below right: *Aphrodite Fritillary.*

COMMON NAME Aphrodite Fritillary

FAMILY Brushfooted Butterflies

GROUP Fritillaries

Speyeria (formerly Argynnis)
Genus

Speyeria atlantis
▶ Atlantis Fritillary

(Formerly called the Mountain Silverspot.) This species is smaller than *S. aphrodite*. It has narrower wings, darker at the base on both the upper and lower sides. The submarginal band below is pale yellow, narrow, distinct, and always present. The wing expanse is 2.25 to 2.5 inches.

It ranges from Quebec to Alberta and southward, but is confined to the Appalachian mountain ranges in southern Pennsylvania and West Virginia.

Near Cresson, on the summit of the Allegheny Mountains, there was a field surrounded by woodland in which violets grew. When the clover was in bloom, myriad Fritillaries, belonging to the species aphrodite, cybele, and atlantis, all congregated there.

Speyeria hydaspe
▶ Hydaspe Fritillary

Many of the western species do not have the spots on the underside silvered, but are none the less beautiful for that. This is one of these species without silvery spots, the spots being creamy white, without metallic luster. The wings of the two sexes are quite alike on the underside. The uppersides are bright tan, dark at the base, marked with heavy, black, confluent spots. There are nearly a dozen species of

Speyeria belonging to the same group with *S. hydaspe*, but this latter is the most beautiful of all of them. Its wing expanse is 2.2 to 2.4 inches. Hydaspe is found in Washington state and British Columbia.

Hydaspe Fritillary in a plate from the original Holland book.

Above right: *Atlantis Fritillary showing the gray-blue eyes that help to distinguish it from Great Spangled Fritillary and Aphrodite Fritillary, which both have brown eyes*
Below right: *Atlantis Fritillary upperside.*

COMMON NAME Atlantis Fritillary

FAMILY Brushfooted Butterflies

GROUP Fritillaries

COMMON NAME Hydaspe Fritillary

FAMILY Brushfooted Butterflies

GROUP Fritillaries

Family

Boloria (formerly Brenthis)
Genus

The Little Fritillaries. Small or medium-sized butterflies, closely resembling those of the genus *Speyeria*. The chief difference is that in *Boloria* only the first subcostal nervule branches off before the end of the cell, while in *Speyeria* the first and second both branch.

The palpi are not so stout, and the basal spur of the median vein of the forewing found in *Speyeria* is missing in *Boloria*. The eggs are subconical, twice as wide as high, truncated, and vertically ribbed. The caterpillars are like those of *Speyeria*, in that they are dark in color, spiny, with the first segment having the longest spines. The chrysalis is pendant, about 0.6 inch long with two rows of conical tubercles on its back. Sixteen species are found in North America, all but the following two of which are subarctic or occur on high mountains.

Boloria selene
▶ Silver-bordered Fritillary

The eggs are pale greenish-yellow. The caterpillar, a dark olive-brown marked with lighter green, is about 0.87 inch long when fully grown, covered with fleshy tubercles. The chrysalis is yellowish-brown marked with darker brown spots, some having a pearly lustre. The undersides of the wings have silvery spots, giving the Silver-bordered Fritillary its name. Wing expanse is 1.40 to 1.70 inches. Its range is from Alaska to Nova Scotia and southward to the mountains of the Carolinas.

Boloria bellona
▶ Meadow Fritillary

This is the only species of the genus, except *B. selene*, found in the densely settled portions of the continent. It is easily distinguished from *B. selene* by the absence of silvery spots on the underwings, and generally found in the late summer and fall of the year, when asters are in bloom. The wing expanse is 1.65 to 1.80 inches. It is common throughout Canada and the northern United States as far west as the Rocky Mountains and south to the Carolinas.

Above right: *Meadow Fritillary on goldenrod.*
Below right: *Meadow Fritillary.*

COMMON NAME Silver-bordered Fritillary
FAMILY Brushfooted Butterflies
GROUP Fritillaries

COMMON NAMES Meadow Fritillary
FAMILY Brushfooted Butterflies
GROUP Fritillaries

Euphydryas (formerly Melitœa)
Genus

The Checkerspots are small to medium-sized butterflies. The palpi are not swollen, the third joint is finely pointed and they are clothed with long hairs. The antennæ are about half as long as the costal margin of forewing, ending with a short, heavy, spoon-shaped knob. The cell in the forewing is closed, in the hindwing it is open. The wings are never silvered on the underside.

The eggs are subconical, flattened on top, fluted on the sides. The caterpillars are gregarious when young, then separating to feed upon the *Scrophulariacœ*, *Castilleja*, and allied plants. They are cylindrical, covered with short spines set with diverging hairs. The chrysalis is rounded at the head, with sharply pointed tubercles on the back. It is white or pale gray, adorned with dark markings and orange spots on the back.

There are several species in the north temperate zone. Most of the species in North America are confined to the western part of the continent, only two being found east of the Mississippi.

Euphydryas phaeton
▶ **Baltimore Checkerspot**

The eggs are brownish-yellow when laid, changing to crimson, and later to black. They get deposited in clusters on balmony (*Chelone glabra*). Hatching in early fall, the little caterpillars spin a web or tent of silk, where they pass the winter. When spring comes, they scatter, start to feed, and after the fifth moult turn into chrysalids, from which the butterflies soon emerge. This is one of the larger species,

the male having a width of 1.75 to 2.00 inches, the female 2.00 to 2.60 inches. They are found locally in colonies in swampy places, where balmony or plantain grows, from Quebec to west of Lake Superior and south to the Carolina mountains.

Above: *Baltimore Checkerspot underside.*
Above right: *Baltimore Checkerspot resting on a grass stem.*
Below right: *Baltimore checkerspot—pupa.*

COMMON NAME Baltimore Checkerspot

FAMILY Brushfooted Butterflies

GROUP Checkerspots

Chlosyne (formerly Melitœa)
Genus

Part of the Checkerspot group. This genus is generally smaller than the *Euphydryas*, but in most other particulars they resemble the preceding genus.

Chlosyne harrisii
▶ Harris' Checkerspot

This butterfly is tan on the upperside of the wings, with the base of the wings and outer margins black. The black margins are widest at the apex. It has five tan spots in the cell of the forewing, two below it, and two white spots on the apex.

   The eggs are lemon-yellow, conical, ribbed, and flattened at the top. The adult caterpillar is reddish, with a black stripe on the middle of its back and nine rows of black, branching spines on the body. On each segment there is a black band in front of the spines, and two black bands behind them. Foodplant's: *Aster Umbellatus*, flat-topped Aster and *Diplopappus*. The chrysalis is pale gray or white, blotched with dark brown. The wing expanse is 1.5 to 1.75 inches. It ranges from Nova Scotia to Lake Superior.

Chlosyne nycteis
▶ Silvery Checkerspot

(Formerly *Phyciodes nycteis*.) Easily mistaken on the wing for *Chlosyne harrisii*, which it closely resembles on the upperside, and with which it is often found flying. However, an examination of the underside at once reveals the difference. The redder forewings, paler

hindwings, and the crescent on the lower outer border of these are marks which cannot be mistaken. The wing expanse in the male is 1.25 to 1.65 inches; in the female, 1.65 to 2.00 inches. Its range is from Maine to the Carolinas and westward to the Rocky Mountains.

Silvery Checkerspot in a plate from the original Holland book.

Above right: *Harris' Checkerspot on oxeye daisy.*
Below right: *Harris' Checkerspot on burdock.*

COMMON NAME Harris' Checkerspot

FAMILY Brushfooted Butterflies

GROUP Checkerspots

COMMON NAME Silvery Checkerspot

FAMILY Brushfooted Butterflies

GROUP Checkerspots

Phyciodes
Genus

The Crescents are usually quite small butterflies, the species found in our region being some shade of tan or reddish above, with dark markings that are less distinctly reproduced on the paler underside of the wings. Of the spots on the underside, the most characteristic is the crescent between the ends of the second and third median nervules. This, when present, is pearly white or silvery in color. Structurally these insects differ most markedly from the preceding genus in the enlarged second joint and the fine, very sharp third joint of the palpi. The eggs are higher than wide, slightly ribbed on top and pitted below, giving them a thimble-like appearance.

The caterpillars are cylindrical, with rows of short tubercles, much shorter than the spines in *Melitœa*, dark in color, marked with paler longitudinal stripes. The chrysalis, with head slightly bifid or two-lobed, is generally pale in color, blotched with brown. Numerous species occur in Central and South America, but only about a dozen in the United States and Canada, most of them in the Southwestern states.

Phyciodes tharos
▶ Pearl Crescent

A very common little butterfly, which everybody must have noticed in late spring or early summer flitting about lawns and gardens, and in fall abounding upon clumps of asters. It may easily be recognized from the illustrations. Wing expanse from 1.25 to 1.65 inches. The variety *marcia* comes from larvæ that have hibernated during the winter, and is lighter and brighter in color, especially beneath, than butterflies of the late summer and fall broods. The greenish-yellow eggs are laid on asters and related plants. Matured caterpillars are dark brown, dotted on the back with yellow; adorned with short, bristly, black spines, yellow at base. The chrysalis is pale gray, blotched with spots of brown. It ranges from southern Labrador to Florida and westward to the Pacific Coast.

Above right: *Pearl Crescent basking on a rock.*
Below right: *Mating Pearl Crescents showing crescent mark on underside of hindwing.*

COMMON NAME Pearl Crescent

FAMILY Brushfooted Butterflies

GROUP Crescents

Family

Phyciodes campestris
▸ **Field Crescent**

(Formerly called *Phyciodes pratensis*, Meadow Crescent.) Resembling *P. tharos*, but the forewings are not as curved on the costal margin, and relatively longer and narrower; the pale markings are more whitish, not so red, and more clearly defined. On the underside, there are no black spots or borders as in *P. tharos*. Wing expanse is 1.15 to 1.40 inches. It ranges from Oregon to southern California, Arizona, and northern Mexico.

Phyciodes picta
▸ **Painted Crescent**

The undersides of the forewings have a band of red on the median area, with the base, costa, apex, and outer margin all pale yellow. The dark spots on this wing stand out prominently. The hindwings beneath are nearly uniformly bright yellow. The wings above are similar to *P. phaon*, but with the light bands of the forewings more pronounced. The larvæ feed on asters. Wing expanse is 0.8 to 1.25 inches. Ranges from Nebraska as far as Mexico.

Phyciodes phaon
▸ **Phaon Crescent**

Note: This particular species does not appear in Holland's book but it is representative of its group and the editor has chosen to include it here.

Above: *Phaon Crescent. A common southern crescent.*
Right: *Phaon Crescent underside.*

COMMON NAME Field Crescent

FAMILY Brushfooted Butterflies

GROUP Crescents

COMMON NAME Painted Crescent

FAMILY Brushfooted Butterflies

GROUP Crescents

COMMON NAME Phaon Crescent

FAMILY Brushfooted Butterflies

GROUP Crescents

Family

Phyciodes
Genus

These butterflies are losely allied to *Phyciodes*, but are distinguished from it by having the forewing more or less deeply excavated on the outer margin about its middle, and the light spots on the hindwings arranged in regular bands. There are also differences in the form of the chrysalids and caterpillars. The genus is best represented in Central and South America, where there are many very beautiful species. Only three occur in our region. We have figured two of these. The genus *Phyciodes* is undoubtedly one of those which originated in the warm neotropical regions and which since the glacial epoch have spread northward. Many of our genera have come to us from the South.

externally like the forewings. The light spots of the upperside reappear on the lower side, but not so distinctly. Wing expanse is 1.25 to 1.75 inches. It ranges through Texas into Mexico and South America.

Cuban Crescent in a plate from the original Holland book.

Phyciodes frisia
▶ **Cuban Crescent**

(Formerly Poey's Crescent.) Below, the wings of this butterfly are tan mottled with dark brown and white, and the spots of the upperside reappear as white bands and markings. Wing expanse is 1.4 to 1.5 inches. It is found in the extreme south of Florida around Key West and is not uncommon in the Antilles, Mexico, and Central America.

Phyciodes texana
▶ **Texan Crescent**

The forewings of this butterfly are tan at the base and broadly marked with dark brown beyond the middle. The hindwings are marbled wood-brown at the base, and dark

Above right: *Texan Crescent nectaring on blue Eupatorium flowers.* **Below right:** *Texan Crescent nectaring on blue Eupatorium flowers.*

COMMON NAME Cuban Crescent

FAMILY Brushfooted Butterflies

GROUP Crescents

COMMON NAME Texan Crescent

FAMILY Brushfooted Butterflies

GROUP Crescents

Family

Chlosyne (formerly Synchloë)
Genus

The Patch-spots. These butterflies are medium-sized or small butterflies, often very brightly colored. Their wings are generally more elongated (the point of the forewing extends further out) than in the two foregoing genera, more excavated on the outer margin of the primaries, and the third joint of the palpus is spindle-shaped, not sharp like the point of a needle, as in *Phyciodes*. The lower discocellular vein in the forewing is straight and not angled, as in the two last-named genera. The eggs, which are laid in clusters on sunflowers (*Helianthus*), are like those of *Phyciodes* in general appearance; the caterpillars and chrysalids like those of *Melitœa*. There are many species of the group found in the American tropics, and among them are many curious mimetic insects, which resemble miniature *Heliconians* and *Ithomiids*. Three species occur in our southland.

Chlosyne janais
▸ Crimson-patch

The upper forewing markings are reproduced underneath. The uppersides of the hindwings are black at the base and on the outer third, enclosing a crimson patch for which this butterfly was named. The middle of the hindwing underside is crossed by a yellow bar with numerous black spots and edged with crimson. There is a marginal row of yellow and a limbal row of white spots parallel to the outer border. Wing expanse is 2.50 to 3.00 inches. Ranges through southern Texas, Mexico, and Central America.

Chlosyne lacinia
▸ Bordered Patch

Note: This particular species does not appear in Holland's book but it is representative of its group and the editor has chosen to include it here.

Crimson-patch in a plate from the original Holland book.

Right: *Not mentioned in Holland, the Bordered Patch is a common and variable species found from the southwestern states south to Argentina.*

COMMON NAME Crimson-patch

FAMILY Brushfooted Butterflies

GROUP Patches

COMMON NAME Bordered Patch

FAMILY Brushfooted Butterflies

GROUP Patches

Polygonia (formerly Grapta)
Genus

The Angle-wings. These are medium-sized or small butterflies. The forewing is strongly curved and pointed at the end of the upper radial, and deeply sculpted on the outer and inner border. The hindwing is tailed at the end of the median nervule. The cells on both wings are closed. The palpi are heavily scaled underneath. The uppersides of the wings are tawny with darker spots, while the undersides mimic the color of bark and dead leaves, often with a silvery spot at about the middle of the hindwing. These butterflies hibernate in winter.

The eggs are taller than they are broad, with a few longitudinal ribs, they taper at the top, which is flat. They are laid in clusters, or strung together, making them look like beads. The larva has a squarish head and cylindrical body, with branching spines. The wood-brown or greenish chrysalid has a head that is bifid or two-lobed. There is a prominent tubercle on the back of the thorax and two rows of dorsal tubercles that are compressed laterally in the thoracic region. The caterpillars feed on the nettle family, including the elm and hops, though willows, azalea, and wild currants are eaten by different species. The genus is confined to the northern temperate zone and there are about a dozen species in America.

Polygonia interrogationis
▶ Question Mark

This is the largest species of the genus. The species is dimorphic, having two forms. In the form *fabricii* (the winter form), the upper sides of the hindwings are a bright tan with dark markings. In the form *umbrosa* (the summer form), they are uniformly dark, except at the base. In the mid-States it is double-brooded, with the second brood hibernating in the winged form. Wing expanse is 2.50 inches. Found in the eastern half of the United States, from southern Canada down through Texas into Mexico.

Above right: *Question Mark underside showing silvery "question mark." This individual is sipping sap from a tree wound.*
Below right: *This is the winter form of the Question Mark.*

COMMON NAME Question Mark

FAMILY Brushfooted Butterflies

GROUP Commas

Polygonia (formerly Grapta)
Genus

Polygonia comma
▶ Eastern Comma

Like the Question Mark, this species is also dimorphic. The summer form is darker, with the wings a deeper orange and the hindwings almost black above. The winter form is lighter in color, with more yellow spots on the upper wings. The larvæ feed on nettles, and some are almost snow-white. Wing expanse is 1.75 to 2.00 inches. The range is much the same as that of the Question Mark.

Polygonia faunus
▶ Green Comma

Readily recognized by the deep indentations of the hindwings, the heavy black border of the upper surface, and the dark tints of the underside mottled conspicuously with paler shades, some variations with green, giving the effect of lichened bark. The wing expanse is 2.00 to 2.15 inches. The larva feeds on willows. Ranges from New England and Ontario to the Carolinas, and westward to the Pacific.

Above: *Green Comma, expertly camouflaged—perched head down with the straight line of the antennae and leading edge of the wing the only visible clues to its presence.* **Above right:** *Summer form of the Eastern Comma.* **Below right:** *Underside of the Eastern Comma showing silvered "comma" mark, swollen at both ends in this species.*

COMMON NAME Eastern Comma

FAMILY Brushfooted Butterflies

GROUP Commas

COMMON NAME Green Comma

FAMILY Brushfooted Butterflies

GROUP Commas

Polygonia (Formerly Grapta)
Genus

Just as the genus *Speyeria* is difficult, the genus *Polygonia* provokes discussion among those who have not had opportunity to study full series of the various species. The resemblances are great and the differences are not accentuated, so the superficial observer is easily confused. The differences are valid, however, even on the upper side of the specimens, which are more nearly alike than the lower side.

Take the species presented on these four pages. They resemble each other closely, but the student will soon see that there are differences, and these are constant. On the underside they are very great. In these species at the end of the cell of the hindwing, on the underside, is a silvery spot that has the form of an inverted L, or is rudely comma-shaped.

Above: *Underside of Gray Comma showing typical camouflage, and thin, hooked "comma."* **Right:** *Gray Comma.*

Polygonia progne
▶ Gray Comma

(Formerly, Currant Angle-wing.) Somewhat smaller than any of the foregoing species. Forewings light bright tan shading into yellow outwardly. The dark markings are smaller than in the other species, but pronounced and clearly defined. Wings below very dark, sprinkled with lighter scales. The larva feeds upon all kinds of plants belonging to the currant family. Wing expanse is 1.85 to 2.00 inches. Ranges from Siberia to Nova Scotia, and from there south to the latitude of Pennsylvania.

COMMON NAME Gray Comma

FAMILY Brushfooted Butterflies

GROUP Commas

Nymphalis (formerly Vanessa)
Genus

The Tortoiseshells. Butterflies in this genus are of medium size. Their eyes are hairy and their palpi are somewhat heavily scaled. The cell of the forewings may or may not be closed, but that of the hindwing is always open. The forewings are more or less excavated around the middle and somewhat elongated at the ends of the upper radial and first median, but not as strongly as in the hindwings of the *Polygonia*. The outer margin is toothed at the ends of the veins and strongly produced at the end of the third median nervule.

The eggs are short, ovoid, tapering above and having a few narrow longitudinal ribs, which increase in depth upward. They are laid in large clusters. The caterpillars, when mature, are cylindrical with longitudinal rows of branching spines, and feed upon elms, willows, and poplars. The chrysalis is not unlike that of *Polygonia*.

The genus is restricted to the north temperate zone and the colder mountain regions of subtropical lands. The butterflies hibernate, and are among the first to be seen in the springtime.

Nymphalis antiopa
▶ Mourning Cloak

This familiar butterfly occurs everywhere in the north temperate zone. Its eggs are laid in large masses on willows, poplars, and elms and in the Middle States there are two broods, the second hibernating in the winged state under eaves and in hollow trees. The wing expanse is 2.75 to 3.25 inches. There is a rare variety of this insect in which the yellow border becomes broad, reaching the middle of the wings.

Above: *Mourning Cloak underside.* **Right:** *Mourning Cloak basking in the sun on a warm spring day.*

COMMON NAME Mourning Cloak

FAMILY Brushfooted Butterflies

GROUP Tortoiseshells

Nymphalis (formerly Vanessa)
Genus

Nymphalis vaualbum
▶ **Compton Tortoiseshell**

(Formerly Nymphalis j-album.) The wings of this butterfly, are patchy black, gold, and warm brown. Its wing expanse is 2.60 to 2.75 inches. The larva feeds upon willows. Confined to the northern parts of the country, ranging up to Labrador in the east and to Alaska in the northwest.

Nymphalis milberti
▶ **Milbert's Tortoiseshell**

This butterfly is easily distinguished by the broad yellow submarginal band on both wings, shaded outwardly by red. Wing expanse is 1.75 inches. The larva feeds upon nettles. Found at high elevations in the Appalachian highlands, ranging northward to Nova Scotia and Newfoundland, thence westward to the Rocky Mountains and the Pacific Coast, its distribution being determined by temperature and the presence of its food plant, though its distribution seems to be more dependent upon climate than upon food, as nettles abound in the Southern States, where the insect is never found.

In addition to these three species of *Nymphalis*, it should be mentioned that there is a very pretty species, known as *Nymphalis californica*, which occurs upon the Pacific Coast. In southern California it is only found on the mountains, but around Vancouver and elsewhere in British Columbia it occurs at sea level. It is a pugnacious little thing, and fights at sight any other butterfly that comes near. The food plant of the larva is *Ceanothus thyrsiflorus*. In the spring, the butterfly delights in feeding on the gum of *Abies concolor*, when it is still fluid.

*Above right: Milbert's Tortoiseshell. Both these species overwinter as adults. **Below right:** Compton Tortoiseshell.*

COMMON NAME Compton Tortoiseshell

FAMILY Brushfooted Butterflies

GROUP Tortoiseshells

COMMON NAME Milbert's Tortoiseshell

FAMILY Brushfooted Butterflies

GROUP Tortoiseshells

The Red Admiral and The Painted Ladies. These butterflies are like those of the last genus in the structure of their wings, except that the hindwings are not angulate, and below the hindwings are generally marked with eye-like spots.

The eggs are ovoid, closely resembling that of *Nymphalis*. The larva is like that of *Nymphalis*, but its spines are relatively not so large and not so distinctly branching. The form of the chrysalis is very like that of *Nymphalis*.

The genus includes comparatively few species, but most have a very wide range, *Vanessa cardui* being almost cosmopolitan in its distribution, having a wider range than that of any other butterfly.

A former name of the American Lady butterfly shown on page 66, (*Pyrameis huntera*, Hunter's Butterfly) commemorated a most remarkable American, John Dunn Hunter. Captured by Native Americans in his infancy, he never knew who his parents were and was brought up among the native peoples. Because of his prowess in the chase they called him "The Hunter."

He grew up as Native American but later forsook that life. He took the name of John Dunn, a man who had been kind to him, and went to Europe, where he became the friend of artists, men of letters, and scientists. He was a favorite with the English nobility and with the King of England. He undertook secure natural history collections from America for certain of his acquaintances. Fabricius named the beautiful insect *Pyrameis huntera*, Hunter's Butterfly, in his honor.

His *Memoirs of Captivity Among the Indians* are well worth reading, and in the charming book, *Coke of Norfolk and His Friends*, there are some most interesting reminiscences.

Vanessa atalanta
▶ Red Admiral

This familiar butterfly is found throughout temperate North America, Europe, northern Africa, and temperate Asia. Its wing expanse is 2.00 to 2.50 inches. The larva feeds on the leaves of hop vines, on nettles, and *Bœhmeria*.

Above right: *Red Admiral perching head downward to feed on sap.* **Below right:** *Red Admiral nectaring on a fall dandelion.*

COMMON NAME Red Admiral

FAMILY Brushfooted Butterflies

GROUP Admirals and Relatives

Vanessa (formerly Pyrameis)
Genus

Vanessa virginiensis
▸ American Lady

(Formerly *Pyrameis huntera*, Hunter's Butterfly.) Marked much like *V. cardui*, but easily discriminated from it by the two large eye-like spots on the underside of the hind wings. The American Lady caterpillar feeds on cud-weed (*Gnaphalium*) and *Antennaria*. Its wing expanse is 2.00 inches. It ranges from Nova Scotia to Mexico and Central America, being comparatively rare in California, but more abundant east of the Sierras.

Vanessa cardui
▸ Painted Lady; Thistle Butterfly

The Painted Lady is easily distinguished from the preceding by the numerous and much smaller eye-spots forming a band on the underside of the hindwings. The caterpillars feed on various species of thistles, nettles, and marshmallows. Its wing expanse is 2.00 to 2.25 inches. This species is found all over the world, except in the tropical jungles of equatorial lands.

Above: *American Lady.* **Below:** *Painted Lady, one of the most widespread of all butterflies.* **Right:** *American Lady nectaring on an aster. Note the two large eyespots on hindwing underside.*

COMMON NAME American Lady

FAMILY Brushfooted Butterflies

GROUP Admirals and Relatives

COMMON NAME Painted Lady; Thistle Butterfly

FAMILY Brushfooted Butterflies

GROUP Admirals and Relatives

Family

Junonia
Genus

The Buckeyes (formerly Peacock Butterflies.) These are medium-sized butterflies with eye-spots on the upper side of the wings. Venation is almost exactly like that of the genus *Vanessa*, save for the fact that the cell of the forewing is usually open. The cell of the hindwing is always open.

The egg is broader than high, flattened on top and adorned by ten very narrow and low vertical ribs. The caterpillars are cylindrical, longitudinally striped, with several rows of branching spines. The chrysalis is arched on the back, curved inwardly in front, and some-what bifid or divided into two at its head, with the two projections rounded.

There are about twenty species in this genus, but most are found in the tropics. Three occur in our region, two of them mostly found in the extreme south.

Junonia cœnia
▶ **Common Buckeye**

The distinctive, eye-like spots occurring on the upper side of the wings reappear on the lower side, but are much smaller, especially on the hindwings. Its wing expanse is 2.00 to 2.25 inches. The larva feeds most commonly on plantains (*Plantago*), snapdragons (*Antirrhinum*), and *Gerardia*. This butterfly is very common in the Southern states, ranging as far north as New England, west to the Pacific, and south into South America.

Above: *Underside of a Common Buckeye nectaring on white sweet clover (Melilotus alba).* **Above right:** *The Common Buckeye can vary in coloration from gray to rich brown.* **Below right:** *Common Buckeye resting on damp sand, where it is often seen.*

COMMON NAME Common Buckeye

FAMILY Brushfooted Butterflies

GROUP Buckeyes

Anartia
Genus

The butterfly is medium-sized, having a weak, hovering flight, and staying near the ground. The second joint of the palpi is thick, the third joint tapering and lightly clothed with scales. The forewings are rounded at the apex, with the outer and inner margins lightly excavated. The cells of the forewing are sometimes closed by a feeble lower discocellular vein (Plate B, Fig 9), which often is missing, leaving the cell open. The outer margin of the hindwings is sinuous, jutting at end of third median nervule, and the cell is open. First and second subcostal nervules in the forewing are fused with the costal.

There are four species of this genus, one of which occurs in the United States, the rest being found in tropical America.

Anartia jatrophæ
▶ White Peacock

The upper wings are whitish, with golden-tan and brown markings, most distinctive being the dark-brown eye-spots. The outer margins of both forewings and hindwings have an almost orange tinge. The underside of the wings is similar to the markings of the uppers, but more muted, with grayish-tan tracings on white, and the outer margins golden. The thorax has a greenish cast. Wing expanse is 1.75 to 2.00 inches. This insect occurs in Florida and Texas and ranges as far south as Argentina.

White Peacock in a plate from the original Holland book.

Right: *Mating White Peacocks.*

COMMON NAME White Peacock

FAMILY Brushfooted Butterflies

GROUP Tropical Brushfoots

Family

The Bag-veins. These are small, delicate butterflies with elongated forewings, which have the costal vein much swollen near the base, somewhat as in the *Satyrinæ*. The upper discocellular vein is lacking in the forewing, and the cell is feebly closed. On the hindwing, the cell is open and the outer margin is slightly crenulate, or crinkled. The two radials spring from a common point.

Mestra amymone
▸ Common Mestra

(Formerly *Cystineura amymone*, Texas Bag-vein.) On the underside the gray markings of the upper side are replaced by yellow, and on the hindwings there is a transverse white band near the base and an incomplete row of white spots on the limbal area. Wing expanse is 1.50 inches. Its range is from Kansas southward through Texas into Central America.

Above: *Common Mestra.*

COMMON NAME Common Mestra

FAMILY Brushfooted Butterflies

GROUP Tropical Brushfoots

Diaethria
Genus

The Leopard-spots. Small butterflies; the upper side of the wings dark in color marked with bands of metallic blue or silvery green, the lower side more or less brilliantly colored, the forewings of some shade of crimson or yellow, banded near the apex, the hindwings silvery white or some pale tint, with circular bands of black enclosing round or pear-shaped black spots.

There are about thirty-five species of the genus thus far known, all of which are found south of our limits, except the one we figure.

Diaethria anna
▸ Leopard-spot

(Formerly *Callicore clymena*.) Found in Florida, but though quite common farther south, appears to be rather local and rare in the peninsula. Wing expanse 1.75 inches.

Above: *The Leopard Spot is a tropical butterfly that wanders to Florida and south Texas. It is called "Eighty-eight" because of its underwing markings.*

Upperwing view of the Leopard-spot in a plate from the original Holland book.

COMMON NAME Leopard-spot

FAMILY Brushfooted Butterflies

GROUP Tropical Brushfoots

Limenitis (formerly Basilarchia)
Genus

The White Admirals and Viceroy. Rather large butterflies. Forewings subtriangular, rounded at the apex, and lightly excavated on the lower two thirds of the outer margin. Hindwings are rounded and somewhat crenulate. The egg is nearly spherical (see Plate C, Fig. f), pitted with large hexagonal cells. The caterpillar in its mature state is cylindrical, with the second segment adorned with two prominent club-shaped tubercles, and the fifth, ninth, and tenth segments also having raised tubercles (see Plate C, Fig. h).

They feed upon birches, willows, poplars, and occasionally oaks, lindens and others. The caterpillars after hatching hibernate in little winter quarters, which they make out of the fragment of a small leaf that they tie together with silken threads and secure to a twig by a few strands. They do not pupate until summer has come. The chrysalis has a projecting boss on the back and its head is either rounded or slightly bifid. The butterflies take wing when the lindens bloom.

There are a number of species in the United States, several of which mimic other butterflies in a singular manner, Viceroy closely resembling Monarch.

Limenitis arthemis astyanax
▶ Red-spotted Purple

On the lower side the wings are brown, banded with black on the margins, the inner row of marginal spots being red, with two red spots at the base of the forewings, and four such spots at the base of the hindwings. The palpi are white below, and there is a white stripe along the sides of the abdomen.

The egg and caterpillar are shown on Plate C. The caterpillar is found on a variety of plants, but most commonly on poplars, wild cherry trees, and aspens. Wing expanse is 3.00 to 3.25 inches. They are found all over the United States and Canada, as far west as the Rocky Mountains, but not in the very hot lowlands of the Gulf region, and are said to occur on the uplands of Mexico.

Above right: *Red-spotted Purple underside.*
Below right: *Red-spotted Purple 'puddling' on gravel.*

COMMON NAME Red-spotted Purple

FAMILY Brushfooted Butterflies

GROUP Tropical Brushfoots

Between *L. astyanax* and the following species, *L. arthemis*, there is more or less affinity. They represent two lines of evolution from a common ancestry, and there are evidences of atavic reversion to type constantly occurring in both forms. They even occasionally interbreed with each other, and hybrids are not altogether uncommon. The whole genus in fact is in a more or less plastic state, and well deserves the careful attention of biologists.

Limenitis arthemis
▸ White Admiral

(Formerly Banded Purple.) It will be seen that there are red spots on the hindwings behind the white band. There is a variety called *proserpina* in which the white band becomes very narrow and the red spots almost or entirely disappear. When the white band and the red spots wholly disappear, as they sometimes do, it is almost impossible to distinguish this species from the Red-spotted Purple.

The egg has "kite-shaped" cells. The caterpillar feeds on birches, aspen, hawthorns, and wild apple and plum trees. Wing expanse is 2.50 to 2.75 inches.

This butterfly is found in Canada, New England, and southward in Pennsylvania upon the higher ranges of the mountains. It is a northern form. It has not thus far been recorded from the western half of the continent, where it is replaced by a somewhat similarly marked, but larger species, known as

L. Weidemeyerii. The latter insect is found as far east as western Nebraska and Colorado.

Above: *White Admiral.* **Right:** *White Admiral nectaring on ninebark (Physocarpus opulifolius).*

COMMON NAME White Admiral

FAMILY Brushfooted Butterflies

GROUP Admirals and Relatives

Limenitis archippus
▶ Viceroy

(Formerly *Limenitis disippus*.) Mimics the Monarch *Danaus plexippus*. Range from Canada to the Gulf. This is one of the most striking cases of mimicry that occurs in our fauna.

Above: *Viceroy larva resembles a bird dropping, giving it protection.* **Above right:** *The Viceroy adult closely resembles the Monarch, but has the additional dark line across the hindwing. Monarchs are distasteful to predators, because their larvae eat milkweed. The Viceroy is thought to gain protection by resembling this distasteful species. However, recent research has shown that the Viceroy is distasteful in its own right; its larvae feed on willows, which contain chemical compounds similar to aspirin.* **Below right:** *Viceroy on Queen Anne's lace.*

COMMON NAME The Viceroy

FAMILY Brushfooted Butterflies

GROUP Admirals and Relatives

Asterocampa (formerly Chlorippe)
Genus

The Emperor Butterflies. These are small butterflies generally of some shade of warm tan, with a submarginal row of eye-like spots on the hindwings, and in a few species with a similar spot on the forewings. The apex of the forewing is somewhat truncated, and the lower two thirds slightly excavated. The hindwings are somewhat elongated in the back at the anal angle. The outer margins of the wings are more or less crenulate. The eggs are nearly globular, broad on top and ornamented with eighteen to twenty broad, but low, vertical ribs, between which are delicate crosslines. The eggs are laid in clusters.

The head of the caterpillar is squarish, crowned by two diverging spines on which are many little spinules. On the back of the head there is a frill of spines. The body of the caterpillar is thickest at the middle, tapering fore and aft. The hind pair of pro-legs are long and diverging. These larvae feed on hackberry trees (*Celtis*).

The chrysalis has a very remarkable arrangement of the cremaster, which is disk-like, and studded with hooks. The whole anatomy is so arranged that the pupa, when suspended, hangs with the ventral, or belly side, parallel to the supporting surface.

There are numerous species in the genus, many of them tropical and very brilliant. Only two commonly occur in the northern portions of our territory, the others found within our limits being inhabitants of the Southern states.

Asterocampa celtis
▶ Hackberry Emperor

Underside grayish-purple, with the spots and markings of the upperside reappearing. Female larger, and, as always is the case in the genus, with the forewings not so pointed as in the male, and the ground-color paler. Wing expanse of the male is 1.80 inches, of the female, 2.10 inches. Its range is from New Jersey west and south to the Gulf.

Right: *Hackberry Emperor basking on a dirt road.*

COMMON NAME Hackberry Emperor

FAMILY Brushfooted Butterflies

GROUP Emperors

Family

Asterocampa (formerly Chlorippe)
Genus

Asterocampa clyton
▸ **Tawny Emperor**

A larger species than the Hackberry Emperor; tawnier on the upper side of the wings and lacking the red-ringed eye-spot on the forewing. The female is much larger than the male, paler in color, with the eye-spots on the hindwings black and conspicuous. Wing expanse for males is 2.00 inches, for females 2.50 to 2.65 inches. It occurs rather rarely in New England, and extends westward to Michigan, southward to the Gulf of Mexico.

*Red Emperor in a plate from
the original Holland book.*

Asterocampa flora
▸ **Red Emperor**

(Currently classified as a variation of the above.) This has no red-ringed eye-spot on the forewing. The ground-color on the upper side is bright-reddish tan; the hindwings are not heavily obscured with brown, and the black ocelli stand forth very prominently upon the lighter ground. The hind-wings are more strongly angulated than in any other North American species, and are solidly bordered with black. The wing expanse for males is 1.75 inches, for females 2.35 inches. Ranges from Florida westward along the borders of the Gulf of Mexico to Texas.

Above right: *A pair of mating Tawny Emperors.*
Below right: *Tawny Emperor "sunning."*

COMMON NAME Tawny Emperor

FAMILY Brushfooted Butterflies

GROUP Emperors

COMMON NAME Red Emperor

FAMILY Brushfooted Butterflies

GROUP Emperors

Smyrna blomfildia
▶ **Blomfild's Beauty**

There are only two species of this genus and they closely resemble each other, so that it is hard to tell them apart. The one that occurs in our borders, *Smyrna karwinskii*, Karwinski's Beauty, has the hindwing rounded at the anal angle, the other has the anal angle of the hindwing squared, with a slight tail-like prolongation. On the underside both species are marked in much the same way.

Wing expanse is 3.00 to 3.25 inches. This butterfly occurs in southern Texas and ranges southward into Brazil.

Upperwing view of the Blomfild's Beauty in a plate from the original Holland book.

Right: *Blomfild's Beauty, a tropical species, occasionally found in south Texas, is attracted to rotting fruit.*

COMMON NAME Blomfild's Beauty

FAMILY Brushfooted Butterflies

GROUP Admirals and Relatives

Hamadryas (formerly Ageronia)
Genus

The Crackers or Calicoes. These are medium or moderately large-sized butterflies. The costal and subcostal veins are fused near the base, and the cells of both wings are closed. The upper side of the wings are curiously marked with checkered spots, generally some shade of blue or gray with white. The underside has broader, paler shades: white, yellow, or red.

They are rapid fliers, and alight on the trunks of trees head downward, wings expanded against the bark of the tree. When they fly they make a clicking sound with their wings. The manner in which this sound is produced is a mystery. Bates, in his *A Naturalist on the Amazons*, writes about it but gives no explanation. In my rambles in tropical forests I have heard it as the insects gyrated above my head, but I do not know how the sound is made.

There are about thirty species of the genus in tropical America, two of which are occasionally found in southern Texas.

Hamadryas feronia
▶ Variable Cracker

(Formerly, *Ageronia feronia*, White-skirted Calico.) The ground-color of the underside of the wings is broadly white, while that of the other species in our fauna, *H. fornax* (Yellow Cracker), is yellow. They may thus be easily told apart.

Cracker in a plate from the original Holland book.

Right: *Variable Cracker in typical head down position on tree trunk.*

COMMON NAME Variable Cracker

FAMILY Brushfooted Butterflies

GROUP Crackers

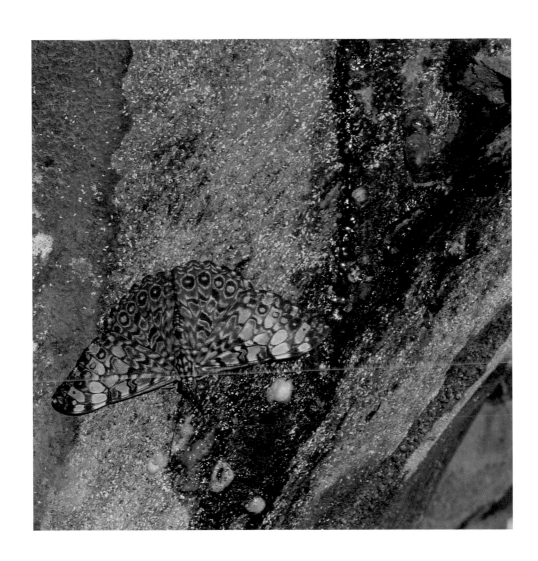

Enodia (formerly Debis)
Genus

The Eyed Nymphs or Pearly-eyes. Holland stated, "Dr. S. H. Scudder set apart the two species we have in our fauna from the Asiatic forms, under the new name *Enodia*, but I have never been able to see any good reason for this, and keep the generic name as it has long stood. The creation of new genera upon the basis of slight differences is to be deprecated and avoided." (Note: This re-classification has remained, so it is represented here.)

This is a large genus, especially well represented in Asia and the Indo-Malayan region.

Creole Pearly-eye in a plate from the original Holland book.

Enodia anthedon
► Northern Pearly-eye

This butterfly has a series of beautiful ocelli on the underside. There is no great difference between the sexes. In the Northern states it is single-brooded, in the South it is double-brooded. Wing expanse is 1.75 to 2.00 inches. The caterpillar feeds on grasses. The insect ranges from Maine to the Gulf, and westward to the Rocky Mountains.

Enodia creola
► Creole Pearly-eye

Easily distinguished from the foregoing by the elongated patches of dark raised scales upon the forewings. Wing expanse is 2.25 inches. The specimen figured is a paratype received from the author of the species.

Ranges from Florida to Mexico along the Gulf.

Above right: *Northern Pearly-eye.*
Below right: *Northern Pearly-eye.*

COMMON NAME Northern Pearly-eye

FAMILY Brushfooted Butterflies

GROUP Satyrs

COMMON NAME Creole Pearly-eye

FAMILY Brushfooted Butterflies

GROUP Satyrs

The Grass-nymphs or Browns. Holland states, "This genus was erected by its author to receive the single species, which we figure. As there is no likelihood of mistaking it for anything else, we forego a long generic description."

More recent research has revealed that there are two *Satyrodes* species, with distinct differences and similarities, but with ranges that overlap only in the northern mid and eastern states. *S. eurydice* is listed as having a "smoky form" in the midwestern parts of the range, having five eye-spots on the underside of the forewing, instead of four.

Satyrodes eurydice
▶ Eyed Brown

(Formerly *Satyrodes canthus*, Grass Nymph.) The caterpillar feeds on grasses, and its early stages and transformations have often been described. The butterfly always haunts meadows and hides among tufts of tall grass in moist places. It has a peculiar jerking flight. Wing expanse is 1.65 to 1.90 inches. It is quite common in New England, the Great Lakes region and Canada, and is found in the cool regions of the Appalachian uplift.

Satyrodes appalachia
▶ Appalachian Brown

This species is very similar to *S. eurydice*, except that the markings on the upper surfaces of the wings show much less contrast. The black eye-spots along the limbal area of the hindwings are not quite so prominent, and the creamy patches on the forewings are subtler in

S. appalachia. Wing expanse is similar to *S. eurydice.* Its range extends from southern New England, south into Virginia, Tennessee, and northern Florida.

Above: *Eyed Brown.* **Right:** *Applachian Brown.*

COMMON NAME Eyed Brown

FAMILY Brushfooted Butterflies

GROUP Satyrs

COMMON NAME Appalachian Brown

FAMILY Brushfooted Butterflies

GROUP Satyrs

Megisto (formerly Neonympha)
Genus

These are small butterflies in the Satyr sub-family. They are rather obscure in color. Both fore- and hindwings are evenly rounded, the forewings with the costal and median veins much swollen at the base. The antennæ are short without a distinctly defined club. The egg is globular, marked with polygonal cells. The caterpillar has a large head, bifid above, and projecting as two cones, thickly studded with little, raised points. The chrysalis is green, comparatively long, pointed at the head, with a blunt tubercle on the thorax.

Some writers maintain that this genus is identical with the genus *Euptychia*, which contains over one hundred species, principally found in the American tropics. Seven species are found in our region.

Upperwing view of the Little Wood-saytr in a plate from the original Holland book.

Megisto cymela
▶ **Little Wood-satyr**

(Formerly, *Neonympha eurytus*.) This butterfly is readily distinguished from the other species in our fauna by the two well-developed eye-spots on the forewings, as well as on the hindwings on the uppe rside. Wing expanse is 1.75 inches. The caterpillar and chrysalis are pale brown, the latter marked with darker brown. It ranges from New England and Ontario to Georgia and westward to Kansas and Texas.

Right: *Little Wood-satyr.*

COMMON NAME Little Wood-satyr

FAMILY Brushfooted Butterflies

GROUP Satyrs

Neonympha
Genus

(Note: According to Holland, the preceding species, *M. cymela*, and both those found below were all grouped in the same genus: *Neonympha*. By current classifications, the following two species are now in different genera. *N. rubricata* now being called *Megisto rubricata*, and *N. sosybius* now termed *Hermeuptychia sosybius*. Their common names have remained the same. From the notes, Holland believed the two below were closely related, so they have been placed together.)

Neonympha rubricata
▶ **Red Satyr**

(Now called *Megisto rubricata*.) This butterfly is most nearly related to *N. sosybius*, but readily distinguished by its much redder color, and by having but one eye-spot on the upper side of the forewing. Wing expanse is 1.40 to 1.75 inches. This species is found in Texas, Arizona, Mexico, and Central America.

Neonympha sosybius
▶ **Carolina Satyr**

(Now called *Hermeuptychia sosybius*.) The upper side of this butterfly is an unspotted, dark mouse-gray. On the underside the wings are paler, crossed by three lines, one defining the basal, the second the median area, and the third just before the outer margin. Between the last two are rows of ocelli (eye-spots), which are obscure, except the first on the forewing and the second and last two on the hindwing. Wing expanse is 1.25 to 1.50 inches. Its range is from the latitude of New Jersey southward through the lower half of the Mississippi Valley to Mexico and Central America.

Red Saytr in a plate from the original Holland book.

Right: *Carolina Satyr, a tiny woodland species well camouflaged among leaves.*

COMMON NAME Red Satyr

FAMILY Brushfooted Butterflies

GROUP Satyrs

COMMON NAME Carolina Satyr

FAMILY Brushfooted Butterflies

GROUP Satyrs

Cœnonympha
Genus

The Ringlets. These are small butterflies. The costal, median, and submedian veins of the forewings are strongly swollen at the base. Both wings are evenly rounded on the outer margin. The eggs are conical, rounded at the bottom, with ribs and cross-lines near the top. The caterpillar has a globular head and cylindrical body, tapering back from the middle, with two cone-like backward projections on the last segment. The chrysalis is straight ventrally, convex dorsally, with a rounded, keeled eminence over the thorax, and a point at the end. It is green or drab, marked with darker spots. Found throughout the north temperate zone. There are a number of species and varieties, most confined to the Pacific Coast and to Alaska.

Cœnonympha tullia
▶ **Common Ringlet**

(Formerly, *Cœnonympha inornata*, Plain Ringlet.) Reddish-gold on the upper side with the outer margin of the forewings and hindwings bathed with a darker shade. On the underside, there is an ocellus or eye-spot near the apex of forewing. On the hindwing, which is dark gray, there is a yellow curved mark beyond the cell and a couple of pale yellow spots near the anal angle. Wing expanse is 1.25 to 1.50 inches. Occurs in Montana, Minnesota, Ontario north of Lake Superior, and eastward to Newfoundland.

Upperwing view of a Common Ringlet in a plate from the original Holland book.

Right: *Common Ringlet nectaring on Rubus.*

COMMON NAME Common Ringlet

FAMILY Brushfooted Butterflies

GROUP Ringlets

The Alpines. Rather small butterflies, dark in color, with eye-spots on the wings, most numerous on the underside. The veins of the forewing are thickened at base, the lower radial in some cases projected into the cell at the point of origin. The outer margin of both wings is evenly rounded. The eggs are sub-conical, ribbed, the ribs often intersecting each other. The larva has a globular head, the body tapering to the back, and the last segment bifurcate. The light brown or ashen-gray chrysalis is convex dorsally and ventrally, humped over the thorax, and wider at the head.

The genus is arctic and confined to the far north, or to the middle higher elevations and summits of high mountains, which have an arctic climate. There are many species in the northern hemisphere, of which we select two for representation.

Erebia discoidalis
▶ Red-disked Alpine

(Formerly, Red-streaked Alpine.) Easily distinguished from all other species in our fauna by its plain, unmarked dark black-brown wings streaked on the costa and suffused over three fourths of the middle of the forewings with deep maroon red. Wing expanse is 1.75 to 2.00 inches. Habitat region is Hudson Bay, westward to Alaska and southward among the snowy peaks of British Columbia. Probably found on high mountains of Idaho and Montana.

Erebia epipsodea
▶ Common Alpine

The underside repeats the markings of the upper side of the wings more or less clearly, and besides has on the hindwing a broad, curved, median, blackish band. Wing expanse is 1.75 to 2.10 inches. This butterfly ranges from the alpine summits of New Mexico northward at suitable mid-high elevations to Alaska, where it is common.

Red-disked Alpine in a plate from the original Holland book.

Above right: *Common Alpine "sunning" in Yellowstone National Park.* **Below right:** *Common Alpine.*

COMMON NAME Red-disked Alpine

FAMILY Brushfooted Butterflies

GROUP Alpines

COMMON NAME Common Alpine

FAMILY Brushfooted Butterflies

GROUP Alpines

Cercyonis (formerly Satyrus)
Genus

The Wood-nymphs. These are medium-sized or small butterflies, with wings marked with eye-spots, or ocelli. On the upper side they are generally very obscurely colored with some shade of gray or brown, occasionally marked by yellow bands. The underside is frequently beautifully streaked and spotted, with the ocelli more prominent than on the uppe rside. The outer margin of the forewing is evenly rounded, that of the hindwing somewhat scalloped. The veins of the forewing are much swollen at the base.

The egg is barrel-shaped, truncated on top, ribbed on the sides, the ribs at the top connected by a waved, raised elevation. The caterpillar has a globular head, a cylindrical body tapering both ways from the middle, and is furnished with diverging anal horns. The chrysalis is green in color, and formed like those of many of the genera belonging to this subfamily. The species in this genus can be very variable.

Upperwing view of the Common Wood-nymph in a plate from the original Holland book.

Cercyonis pegala
▶ Common Wood-nymph

(Formerly Southern Wood-nymph.) Easily recognized by its large size, this butterfly is one of the largest species in our fauna. It is also remarkable for the broad subterminal yellow band on the forewing that is marked in the male by one eye-spot, and in the female by two such spots. Wing expanse is 2.75 to 3.00 inches. This species is found throughout much of the United States.

Right: *Common Wood-nymph (dark form) nectaring on knapweed.*

COMMON NAME Common Wood-nymph

FAMILY Brushfooted Butterflies

GROUP Satyrs

Libytheana
Genus

The Snouts. These are small butterflies, with the palpi enormously elongated in comparison with other butterflies. The forewings are strongly excavated on the outer margin, and projecting at the end of the lower radial. The hindwing is upwardly lobed at the base, excised before the outer angle, and the outer margin is somewhat scalloped.

The egg is ovoid, nearly twice as high as wide, ribbed, every other rib being higher than the one beside it and increasing in height toward the top. The caterpillar has a small head, overarched by the anterior swollen segments. It lives on the hackberry (*Celtis*). The chrysalis has a conical abdomen, the head pointed, with two raised ridges running from the head on either side to the middle of the first segment of the abdomen; between these ridges is a low tubercle.

There are numerous species found in all parts of the world, but only one occurs within our limits.

Libytheana carinenta
▶ **American Snout**

(Formerly *Libytheanæ bachmani*, Common Snout.) This butterfly ranges from New England and Ontario southward and westward as far as Arizona and south into northern Mexico.

Above: *American Snout upper side.* **Right:** *American Snout with closed wings, showing elongated palps producing the "snout."*

COMMON NAME American Snout

FAMILY Brushfooted Butterflies

SPECIES Snouts

Family

Above: *Rounded Metalmark, found in south Texas, beautifully demonstrates metallic wing markings.*

The Metalmarks. Defined by their thread-like metal maskings. There are nearly fifty species of this genus found in the American tropics. There are but two species in the eastern part of the United States, and two others in California. Several stray into south Texas and along our southern borders.

Calephelis perditalis
▶ Rounded Metalmark

Note: This particular species does not appear in Holland's book but it is representative of its group and the editor has chosen to include it here.

COMMON NAMES Rounded Metalmark

FAMILY Gossamer-wing Butterflies

GROUP Metalmarks

Melanis
Genus

Above: *Red-bordered Pixie, a striking metalmark that lacks metallic spots. The Pixie is found locally along the lower Rio Grande.*

Melanis pixe
▶ Red-bordered Pixie

Note: This particular species does not appear in Holland's book but it is representative of its group and the editor has chosen to include it here.

COMMON NAME Red-bordered Pixie

FAMILY Gossamer-wing Butterflies

GROUP Metalmarks

Strymon (formerly Thecla)
Genus

The Hairstreaks. These are mostly small butter-flies. On the upper side of the wings they are very often colored with iridescent blue, green, or purple, sometimes reddish or dark brown. On the underside, the wings are marked with lines and spots variously arranged and often very strikingly colored. What has been said as to the eggs, larvæ, and chrysalids of the family apply as well to this, as to many of the follow-ing genera.

While students of this group have subdi-vided extensively, and with scientific propri-ety have erected a number of genera which are acceptable to specialists, there seems to the writer no need for going into these things in this book, as most of the distinctions drawn are too fine to be appreciated by any but specialists.

Strymon melinus
► **Gray Hairstreak**

(Formerly *Thecla melinus*, Common Hairstreak.) This common little butterfly may easily be recognized by its plain, slaty upper surface, marked by a large black spot crowned with crimson between the origin of the two tails on the hindwings. The caterpillar feeds on a variety of plants, including legumes, mallows, and many other plant families. Wing expanse is 1.10 to 1.20 inches. The insect is found throughout temperate North America, and southward into Mexico and Central America on the highlands.

Above: *Gray Hairstreak, unusual among Hairstreaks, this species will often perch with wings open.*
Right: *Gray Hairstreak, nectaring on knapweed.*

COMMON NAME Gray Hairstreak
FAMILY Gossamer-wing Butterflies
GROUP Hairstreaks

Satyrium edwardsii
▸ **Edwards' Hairstreak**

(Formerly *Thecla edwardsi*, Edwards' Hair-streak.) On the upper side, the wings are dark brown glossed with leaden gray, with a pale sex-mark on the forewing of the male near the costa. The caterpillar feeds on the young leaves of various kinds of oak, particularly scrub oak. Wing expanse is 1.15 inches. The species ranges from Quebec westward to Colorado and is locally common in New England, New York, and western Pennsylvania.

Satyrium calanus
▸ **Banded Hairstreak**

On the upper side this butterfly resembles *S. edwardsi*, but is a warmer brown in color. The undersides of the wings are marked by fine white lines on the outer half, but these lines are not broken as in *S. edwardsi*, but form continuous bands. The wing expanse is 1.15 inches. The larva feeds on oaks. The insect ranges from Quebec to Colorado and Texas, and is common in western Pennsylvania.

Above: *Edwards' Hairstreak. Most hairstreaks perch with their wings closed and so although Holland describes the upper sides that he studied from specimens, the field observer would only see the undersides.* **Right:** *Banded Hairstreak. This individual has recently visited a milkweed flower and has a milkweed pollinium stuck to its foot.*

COMMON NAME Edwards' Hairstreak

FAMILY Gossamer-wing Butterflies

GROUP Hairstreaks

COMMON NAME Banded Hairstreak

FAMILY Gossamer-wing Butterflies

GROUP Hairstreaks

Thecla halesus
▶ Great Purple Hairstreak

The upper side is deep purplish blue, as shown in our figure; on the lower side the thorax is black spotted with white, the abdomen orange-red; the wings warm sepia spotted with crimson at their bases, in the males glossed with a strip of metallic green on the forewings, and in both sexes adorned at the anal angle by spots of metallic green, red, and iridescent blue. Wing expanse is 1.35 to 1.50 inches.

   Common in Central America and Mexico, ranging north through the hotter parts of the Gulf States, and has been recorded from southern Illinois. Occurs in southern California and Arizona. The larva feeds on mistletoe.

Great Purple Hairstreak in a plate from the original Holland book.

Thecla m-album
▶ White-M Hairstreak

Smaller than the preceding species, bluer, and not inclined to greenish at base of wings on upper side; on underside forewing crossed by a submarginal and a median line of white, continued on the hindwings, zigzagged at anal angle so as to look like an inverted M; near this is a rounded crimson patch; anal angle black-glossed with blue. Wing expanse is 1.35 to 1.45 inches. Ranges from New Jersey and Wisconsin to Venezuela.

Right: *White-M Hairstreak. Note the white "M" on the underside, giving this hairstreak its name.*

COMMON NAME Great Purple Hairstreak

FAMILY Gossamer-wing Butterflies

GROUP Hairstreaks

COMMON NAMES White-M Hairstreak

FAMILY Gossamer-wing Butterflies

GROUP Hairstreaks

Satyrium (formerly Thecla)

Satyrium liparops
▶ Striped Hairstreak

This species is dark brown on the upper side. On the underside, the lines are arranged much as in *S. edwardsi*, but farther apart, quite narrow, and scarcely defining the darker bands between them. The spots at the anal angle are obscure and blackish. The wing expanse is 1.15 inches. The larva feeds on oaks, willows, wild plum, and many other plants. The insect ranges from Quebec through the northern Atlantic States as far west as Montana and Colorado, but is never common.

Satyrium acadica
▶ Acadian Hairstreak

The wings on the under side are pale wood-brown, with a black bar at the end of the cells, and submarginal and median bands of small black spots surrounded with white; on the hindwings there is a submarginal row of red crescents, growing smaller from the anal angle toward the outer angle. Near the anal angle are two conspicuous black spots separated by a broad patch of bluish-green scales. Wing expanse is 1.15 to 1.25 inches. The caterpillar feeds on willows. The insect ranges from Quebec to Vancouver Island.

Above right: *Striped Hairstreak.* **Below right:** *Acadian Hairstreak, nectaring on swamp milkweed.*

COMMON NAME Striped Hairstreak
FAMILY Gossamer-wing Butterflies
GROUP Hairstreaks

COMMON NAME Acadian Hairstreak
FAMILY Gossamer-wing Butterflies
GROUP Hairstreaks

Chlorostrymon (formerly Thecla)

Above: *Silver Banded Hairstreak. Its hindwing coloration matches perfectly the brown of the spent Eupatorium blossoms.*

Chlorostrymon simæthis
▸ Silver-banded Hairstreak

(Formerly *Thecla simæthis*, Brown-margined Hairstreak.) Closely resembling in many respects the following species, especially on the upper side, but the white band on the hindwings is straight and the outer margins are heavily marked with bright reddish-brown. Expanse 0.85 to 1.00 inch. This pretty species ranges from Texas well into South America.

COMMON NAME Silver-banded Hairstreak

FAMILY Gossamer-wing Butterflies

GROUP Hairstreaks

Callophrys (formerly Thecla)
Genus

Above: *Juniper Hairstreak is part of a highly variable species complex whose coloration can vary from iridescent green to various shades of brown.*

Callophrys gryneus
▸ "Olive" Juniper Hairstreak

(Formerly *Thecla damon*, Olive Hairstreak.) On the upper side of the form called *discoidalis*, the central part of the forewing is broadly marked with reddish fulvous. The caterpillar feeds on the red cedar (*Juniperus virginiana*). It is double-brooded in the North and triple-brooded in the South. The species ranges from Ontario to Texas over the whole eastern half of the United States.

COMMON NAME "Olive" Juniper Hairstreak

FAMILY Gossamer-wing Butterflies

GROUP Hairstreaks

Callophrys (formerly Thecla)
Genus

Callophrys niphon
▶ **Eastern Pine Elfin**

(Formerly *Thecla niphon*, The Banded Elfin.)
On the upper side the insect is plain reddish-
brown. The caterpillars feed upon pines. The
insect ranges from Nova Scotia to Colorado
in the Northern States, and is only found in
pine woods, but is never very abundant.
Expanse 1.10 inches.

Callophrys henrici
▶ **Henry's Elfin**

(Formerly, *Thecla henrici*, Henry's Hairstreak.)
Very much like the following species, but
with the outer half of the wings washed with
reddish-brown. The hindwings on the underside are blackish-brown; on the basal half of
the outer margin paler, the division between
the dark and light shades being irregular and
sharply defined. Expanse 1.00 to 1.10 inches.
This species, like C. irus, feeds on young
plums. It ranges from Maine to West Virginia,
and is not very common.

Above: *Henry's Elfin occurs with its hostplant, American holly
on the Atlantic coastal plain. Inland its food plants vary.*
Right: *Eastern Pine Elfin nectaring on star toadflax
(Comandra umbellata).*

COMMON NAME Eastern Pine Elfin

FAMILY Gossamer-wing Butterflies

GROUP Elfins

COMMON NAME Henry's Elfin

FAMILY Gossamer-wing Butterflies

GROUP Elfins

Callophrys irus
▶ Frosted Elfin

(Formerly *Thecla irus*, Hoary Elfin.) Grayish-brown on the upper side, on the underside of the same color, but paler on the outer margins and darker toward the base; small crescents appear on the outer margins of the hindwings below, or they may be absent. Wing expanse is 1.10 inches. The larva feeds on wild lupine and wild indigo along the Atlantic to the Pacific and Westward into Texas.

Above: *Frosted Elfin male.* **Right:** *Frosted Elfin female on its host plant, wild lupine.*

COMMON NAME Frosted Elfin

FAMILY Gossamer-wing Butterflies

GROUP Elfins

The Harvester. This insect is small, bright orange-yellow on the upper side, the costal and outer margin of the forewings and the basal half of the hindwings are dark brown. The underside is more or less mottled with gray and brown, with the markings of the upper side reappearing. The egg is sub-globular, much wider than it is high, marked with a multitude of fine and indistinct raised ridges disposed in the form of polygonal cells. The caterpillar is slug-shaped, covered with bristling spines, upon which it gathers the scales of the woolly aphids upon which it feeds. The chrysalis is brown in color, showing a remarkable likeness to the face of a monkey, a phenomenon that also appears in the case of its allies of the genus *Spalgis*, found in Africa and Asia. Only one species of the genus is known.

Above: Harvester male showing upper side of wings. **Above right:** Harvester female laying eggs among woolly aphids on an alder tree. **Below left:** Harvester larva, fully grown and ready to pupate. **Below right:** Harvester pupa on top of an alder leaf and showing its "monkey face."

Feniseca tarquinius
▶ **Harvester**

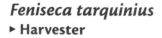

There is considerable variation in the size of the dark markings on the upper side of the wings, and in some specimens they almost entirely disappear. Wing expanse is 1.30 inches. Ranges from Nova Scotia to the Carolinas, and through the Mississippi Valley.

COMMON NAME Harvester

FAMILY Gossamer-wing Butterflies

GROUP Harvesters

Lycaena (formerly Chrysophanus)
Genus

The Coppers. A group of small butterflies with the upperside of the wings some shade of coppery red or orange, often glossed with deep purple. On the underside, the wings are marked with a multitude of spots and lines. The egg is hemispherical, flattened on the base, pitted above with polygonal or circular depressions. The larva is slug-shaped, thickest in the middle and tapering at either end, with a very small head. The chrysalis is rounded at either end, and supported by a silken harness a little in front of the middle. The genus is found in both hemispheres. There are over a dozen species in the United States.

Lycaena phlaeas
▸ American Copper

(Formerly *Chrysophanus hypophlœas.*) This is one of the commonest butterflies in the United States. Holland states, "Everybody has seen it flitting about upon lawns and in gardens." The caterpillar feeds upon common sorrel (*Rumex acetosella*). Wing expanse is 1.00 inch. The insect ranges from Hudson Bay to the Gulf States, but does not invade the hot belt about the Gulf.

Lycaena epixanthe
▸ Bog Copper

(Formerly Least Copper.) The smallest species in the genus, confined to the north. The male above has the wings dusky, shot with violet, with a few red spots near the anal angle of the hind wings. The female is pale gray above,

more profusely marked with dark spots than the male. Below the wings are pale gray sprinkled with bluish scales at the base, marked as above. Wing expanse is 0.85 to 0.95 inch. Common in acid bogs from Newfoundland to British Columbia, never south of New England.

Above: *Bog Copper, a denizen of acid bogs.*
Right: *American Copper, basking in the sunshine.*

COMMON NAME American Copper

FAMILY Gossamer-wing Butterflies

GROUP Coppers

COMMON NAME Bog Copper

FAMILY Gossamer-wing Butterflies

GROUP Coppers

Lycaena (formerly Chrysophanus)
Genus

Lycaena hyllus
▸ Bronze Copper

(Formerly *Chrysophanus thoë*.) The female differs from the male in having the forewings bright coppery red, marked with a number of dark spots, three in the cell, one below it, and an irregular transverse band of them crossing the limbal area. The outer margin is heavily banded with dusky gray. Below the forewing is tawny red in both sexes, pale gray at the apex; the hindwings are bluish-gray with a broad band of carmine on the outer margin. Both wings underneath are profusely adorned with small black spots. Wing expanse is 1.30 to 1.40 inches. Ranges from Maine to Colorado, southward to northern Virginia.

Lycaena helloides
▸ Purplish Copper

The male has the wings on the upperside broadly shot with iridescent purple. The female, which is larger than the male, has red wings, with less iridescence. Below, the forewings in both sexes are pale red, the hindwings reddish-gray with a marginal row of brick-red crescents. Wing expanse is 1.15 to 1.30 inches. It ranges from the Great Lakes area across the northwest to British Columbia.

Above right: *Bronze Copper showing the outer marginal band.*
Below right: *Purplish Copper, near the Great Salt Lake, Utah.*

COMMON NAME Bronze Copper

FAMILY Gossamer-wing Butterflies

GROUP Coppers

COMMON NAME Purplish Copper

FAMILY Gossamer-wing Butterflies

GROUP Coppers

Family

Lycaeides (formerly Lycæna)
Genus

The Blues. The butterflies in this group are generally small, with the upperside being some shade of pale blue. On the underside the wings are paler in color, variously marked with spots and lines.

Holland comments that the genus has been subdivided into smaller subgenera, but as an ability to discriminate these subdivisions involves a knowledge of minuter anatomical details, which is only possessed by specialists, the writer has not deemed it worthwhile in a little manual like this to go deeply into these matters.

The old name *Lycæna*, which has been in vogue for a century, and which is still applied to part of the group, is sufficiently characteristic. If we were reviewing all the species of the world, of which there are many hundreds in this assemblage of forms, we would be forced to use the minuter methods of classification.

The eggs are turban-shaped. The caterpillars are slug-shaped, feeding on the petals and bracts of flowers or tender terminal leaves. The chrysalids are short, rounded at either end, and are supported by a silken harness by which they are closely bound to the supporting surface.

Lycaeides melissa
▶ Melissa Blue

(Formerly *Lycæna melissa*, Orange-margined Blue.) The male on the upperside is pale blue, with a narrow black marginal line and white fringes. The female is brown or lilac-gray with a series of orange-red crescents on the outer margin of both wings. The wings below are stone-gray with the usual spots, but on the hindwings the orange crescents are oblong tipped inwardly with black and outwardly with metallic green. Wing expanse is 0.90 to 1.15 inches. It ranges from Arizona to Montana.

Right: *Melissa Blue was formerly called the Orange-margined Blue," aptly named.*

COMMON NAME Melissa Blue

FAMILY Gossamer-wing Butterflies

GROUP Blues

Family

Lycaeides melissa samuelis
▶ 'Karner' Melissa Blue

(Formerly *Lycæna scudderi*, Scudder's Blue.) The upper side of the male is hard to discriminate from the same sex of *L. melissa*. The female is darker, and has only a few orange crescents on the outer margin of the hindwing on the upper side. On the under side the wings are shining white, the spots much reduced in size, the large orange spots found in *L. melissa* being replaced by little ochreous spots very obscurely tipped externally by a few greenish scales. The caterpillar feeds on lupine and allied plants. The insect is very common in the basin of the St. Lawrence River and the Great Lakes. It abounds in central New York.

Editor's Note: The eastern population has seriously declined since Holland's time. This subspecies is now listed as Federally Endangered.

Above: *'Karner' Melissa Blue female perching on sweetfern (Comptonia peregrina), which was growing near to its larval food plant, wild lupine.* **Right:** *'Karner' Melissa Blue, perching atop a dried clover flowerhead. This is now recognized as a subspecies of the Melissa Blue (p.126).*

COMMON NAME 'Karner' Melissa Blue

FAMILY Gossamer-wing Butterflies

GROUP Blues

Family

Celastrina (formerly Lycæna)
Genus

Celastrina ladon neglecta
▶ Summer Azure

(Formerly *Lycæna pseudargiolus*, Common Blue.) This insect, which is quite common and may be found on the wing from early spring until late in the autumn, illustrates in a remarkable manner the phenomenon of polymorphism. It has a number of forms, some of which are seasonal, some of which are sexual, some of which are climatic.

It is in fact only through the labors of the late William Henry Edwards that some of the mysteries were cleared up, he having by breeding established the fact that some of the so-called species could be raised from eggs derived from one common stock. The great series of specimens upon which his conclusions were founded are in the possession of the writer, and have from time to time been supplemented by a vast amount of other material all of which confirms his teachings.

The forms *lucia* and *marginata* are winter forms, coming from chrysalids which have endured the long cold of the winter months and are the first to appear in spring. They are the only forms which occur in the far north near the Arctic Circle.

The forms *pseudargiolus* and *neglecta* are summer forms of the second and third generations, produced from eggs laid by *lucia* and *marginata*. *Nigra* is a dimorphic female form belonging to the summer broods and is melanic, or a form in which dark color prevails. Students of biology recognize a tendency in some animals to become black, while there is also a tendency to become white, or to produce albinoes. These tendencies in color to opposite directions are often observed in butterflies, and the melanic female of this species is an illustration.

There is still another form, *piasus*, which occurs in Arizona and Mexico, and is climatic, or due to the influence of environment.

The winter forms are dwarfed and darkly marked on the underside. The summer forms are larger, pale on the underside and dark on the outer borders above.

The species has a range in the expanse of wing of from 0.85 to 1.25 inches. It occurs from Alaska to Florida, and from Anticosti to northern Mexico.

Right: *Summer Azure female laying eggs among the flower buds of a spiraea.*

COMMON NAME Summer Azure

FAMILY Gossamer-wing Butterflies

GROUP Blues

Everes (formerly Lycæna)
Genus

Everes comyntas
▶ Eastern Tailed Blue

Somewhat closely resembling the following species, but appreciably smaller. Wing expanse is 1.00 to 1.10 inches. It ranges from Saskatchewan to Costa Rica, and from the Atlantic to the Rocky Mountains.

Everes amyntula
▶ Western Tailed Blue

The male is pale blue on the upperside, and the female is darker. The hindwings are marked with a submarginal row of orange crescents pupilled with black. Wing expanse is 1.00 to 1.25 inches. This butterfly ranges from the Rocky Mountains to the Pacific in British America and southward as far as Colorado.

Above: *Eastern Tailed Blue underside.* **Below:** *Western Tailed Blue underside.* **Above right:** *Eastern Tailed Blue.* **Below right:** *Western Tailed Blue.*

COMMON NAME Eastern Tailed Blue

FAMILY Gossamer-wing Butterflies

GROUP Blues

COMMON NAME Western Tailed Blue

FAMILY Gossamer-wing Butterflies

GROUP Blues

Family

Brephidium isophthalma
▶ **Eastern Pygmy-blue**

(Formerly Dwarf Blue.) The wings are light brown above in both sexes, with a row of dark spots on the outer margin of the hind-wings. Pale brown below, profusely marked by light spots and bands, the dark marginal spots of the upperside reappearing, and defined by circlets of metallic scales. Wing expanse is 0.75 inch. It is found in the Gulf states and the Antilles.

Eastern Pygmy-blues shown actual size; from a plate in the original Holland book.

Brephidium exile
▶ **Western Pygmy-blue**

(Formerly, Pygmy Blue.) The smallest of the North American butterflies. It closely resembles the foregoing, but is distinguished from it by the white spot on the fringe near the inner angle of the forewing, and the white fringes of the same wing near its apex. Wing expanse is 0.65 inch. The Western Pygmy-blue occurs in the Gulf states and in tropical America.

Above right: *Western Pygmy-blue upperside.*
Below right: *Western Pygmy-blue is the smallest butterfly in North America, and possibly the world.*
Left: *Western Pygmy-blues shown actual size; from a plate in the original Holland book.*

COMMON NAME Eastern Pygmy-blue

FAMILY Gossamer-wing Butterflies

GROUP Blues

COMMON NAME Western Pygmy-blue

FAMILY Gossamer-wing Butterflies

GROUP Blues

Leptotes cassius
▶ **Cassius Blue**

(Formerly *Lycæna theona*, West Indian Blue.) The male is shining lavender-blue, and this color also glosses the dark outer borders of the wings. The female is white, with outer borders heavily blackish, the forewings shot with shining sky-blue at the base. The hind-wings near the anal angle have conspicuous eye-spots, both above and below. Wing expanse is 0.80 inch. It occurs in the Gulf states and throughout the tropics of the New World.

Upperside of the Cassius Blue in a plate from the original Holland book.

Leptotes marina
▶ **Marine Blue**

The male is pale dusky lilac on the upperside of its wings, with the dark bands of the underside showing through on the upperside. The female is dark brown above, her wings shot with lilac-blue at the base. The dark bands on the disk are prominent in this sex, especially on the forewings. The larva feeds on alfalfa and allied plants. Wing expanse is 1.10 inches. This species occurs in Texas, Arizona, southern California, and southward.

Above right: *The zebra-striped Marine Blue occurs in the southwest, but occasionally disperses as far north as western New York and southern Ontario.* **Below right:** *Cassius Blue female in the process of egg laying (note curled abdomen.).*

COMMON NAME Cassius Blue

FAMILY Gossamer-wing Butterflies

GROUP Blues

COMMON NAME Marine Blue

FAMILY Gossamer-wing Butterflies

GROUP Blues

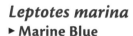

Glaucopsyche (formerly Lycæna)

Glaucopsyche piasus
▶ **Arrowhead Blue**

(Formerly *Lycæna heteronea*, Varied Blue.) The largest species of the blues. The male is blue, the female brown. The markings on the upperside of the latter recalling the female of the modern genus *Lycaena*, the Coppers. Wing expanse is 1.25 to 1.40 inches. Below, the wings are white marked with faint brown spots on the hindwings and more distinct spots on the forewings. It ranges from Colorado to California at suitable elevations among the mountains.

Glaucopsyche lygdamus
▶ **Silvery Blue**

The underside is pale cocoa-brown, having on each wing a submarginal band of black spots encircled with white, with similar spots at the end of the cells, and one or two also on the costa of the hindwing. Wing expanse is 0.85 to 1.00 inch. This blue ranges from Michigan to Georgia.

Female Arrowhead Blue, top; male Arrowhead Blue, bottom; from a plate from the original Holland book.

Above right: *Silvery Blue upperside. A male puddling on a dirt path.* **Below right:** *Silvery Blue, photographed in Yellowstone National Park.*

COMMON NAME Arrowhead Blue

FAMILY Gossamer-wing Butterflies

GROUP Blues

COMMON NAME Silvery Blue

FAMILY Gossamer-wing Butterflies

GROUP Blues

Ascia (formerly Pieris) Genus

The Whites. These are medium-sized butter-flies, generally white in color, and marked on both upper- and undersides with darker lines and spots. The antennæ are clubbed, the palpi short and compressed, with the last joint short and pointed. The eggs are spindle-shaped, with vertical raised ridges. The cater-pillar is elongated, its head hemispherical. It feeds upon cruciferous plants.

The chrysalis attaches by the anal extremity and is held in place by a silk harness. It is con-cave on the ventral side, convex on the dorsal side, with a hump-like or keel-shaped promi-nence over the thorax, and a conical head.

An extensive genus, it is confined princi-pally to the northern hemisphere.

Ascia monuste
▶ Great Southern White

On the underside, the hindwings are grayish saffron yellow, crossed by a poorly defined pale brown transverse band of spots. The veins are pale brown, and between them are pale brown rays on the interspaces. Wing expanse is 1.65 to 2.35 inches. It has a wide range in tropical America, and is common in the Gulf states.

Above: *The blue antennal knobs of the male Great Southern White are diagnostic.* **Right:** *Great Southern White female. This species is highly variable in color.*

COMMON NAME Great Southern White

FAMILY Whites and Sulphurs

GROUP Whites

Pontia (formerly Pieris)
Genus

Above: *Checkered White showing both underside and upperside of wings.*

Pontia protodice
▸ **Checkered White**

(Formerly *Pieris protodice*, Common White.)
Wing expanse is 1.90 to 2.15 inches. Its range
is from the Atlantic to the Rocky Mountains,
and from southern Canada to the Gulf states.

COMMON NAME Checkered White

FAMILY Whites and Sulphurs

GROUP Whites

Family

Pieris
Genus

Above: *A male Mustard White frantically trying to mate with a daisy, that alas, shows no interest!*

Pieris napi
▶ **Mustard White**

This species occurs throughout temperate and boreal North America, ranging well up to the Arctic Circle. It also occurs in the eastern hemisphere, ranging from north Africa to the North Cape, and all over temperate and sub-arctic Asia. The species ranges from the Atlantic to the Pacific, and from Alaska to the northern boundaries of the Gulf states. Wing expanse is 1.50 to 2.00 inches.

COMMON NAME Mustard White

FAMILY Whites and Sulphurs

GROUP Whites

Pieris rapæ
▶ Cabbage White

(Formerly Cabbage Butterfly.) This excessively common insect has been in comparatively recent years introduced from Europe. It first appeared about Quebec in 1860; since then it has come to occupy the continent, and wherever cabbages are grown hundreds of these butterflies may be seen. The loss to gardeners which it causes is estimated to run into millions of dollars annually. It feeds on all the *Cruciferæ*. The multiplication of *P. rapæ* has been followed by the partial extinction of our native Pierids just as our birds have disappeared before the English Sparrow. Wing expanse is 2.00 inches.

Above right: *Cabbage White underside.* **Below right:** *Male Cabbage Whites have a single spot, females two. This appears to be a female with a light second spot.*

COMMON NAME Cabbage White

FAMILY Whites and Sulphurs

GROUP Whites

Family

Above: *West Virginia White nectaring on the flowers of its larval host plant, toothwort (Cardamine diphylla)*

Pieris Virginiensis
▸ West Virginia White

Note: This particular species does not appear in Holland's book but it is representative of its group and the editor has chosen to include it here.

COMMON NAME West Virginia White

FAMILY Whites and Sulphurs

GROUP Whites

Euchloë
Genus

Above: *The beautiful green markings of the Olympia Marble are produced by the combination of yellow scales overlapping black ones.*

Euchloë olympia
▶ Olympia Marble

Above pure white without any red at the tip of the primaries; a transapical black band, broken in the middle, and a small black bar closes the cell. Underside well shown in our figure, showing a faint rosy tint in the hind-wings which is characteristic of the species. It flies only when the sun is shining. Wing expanse 1.35 to 1.40 inches. Found in Texas.

COMMON NAME Olympia Marble

FAMILY Whites and Sulphurs

GROUP Whites

These small yellow butterflies are margined with black. The forewings are somewhat narrow and projected and the antennæ are quite short. The upper radial vein in the forewing is missing. There are three species found in the subtropical regions of the New World, one of which invades our territory.

Nathalis iole
▶ Dainty Sulphur

(Formerly Dwarf Yellow.) This little species cannot be mistaken. The larva feeds on *Erodium cicutarium*, or pin-clover, and other *Geraniaceæ*. Wing expanse is 1.00 to 1.25 inches. It ranges from southern Indiana and Illinois to Arizona, southern California, and northern Mexico.

Above: *Dainty Sulphur.* **Right:** *Dainty Sulphur.*

COMMON NAME Dainty Sulphur

FAMILY Whites and Sulphurs

GROUP Whites

Family

Anthocharis (formerly Euchloë)

The Orangetips and Marble-wings. Small white butterflies with the apex of the forewings dark brown, they are marked with spots and bands of orange-yellow or crimson. On the underside, the hindwings are generally more or less mottled with green spots and streaks. The eggs are spindle-shaped, the caterpillar relatively long, with a small head. The chrysalis has a greatly elongated head area, and the wing-cases are compressed, forming a keel-shaped projection.

Anthocharis sara
▶ **Sara Orangetip**

(Formerly Lucas' Orangetip.) There are numerous varieties of this beautiful insect. On the underside, the hindwings are marked with irregular patches of greenish scales having a "mossy" appearance. Wing expanse is 1.75 inches. It occurs in the Pacific states.

Anthocharis midea
▶ **Falcate Orangetip**

(Formerly *Euchloë genutia*.) These butterflies are readily recognized by the hooked tip of the forewings, although the female has no orange marking on the wing tip. The species is single-brooded in the Northern states, but double-brooded in the Carolinas. Wing expanse is 1.30 to 1.50 inches. The caterpillar feeds on *Sisybrium*, *Arabis*, *Cardamine*, and other cruciferous plants. Its range is from New England to Texas.

Above right: *Sara Orangetip nectaring on rock cress (Arabis). Both Sara and Falcate Orangetips fly early in the spring.* **Below right:** *Falcate Orangetip nectaring on a violet (Viola). This individual shows the orange wingtips characteristic of the male.*

COMMON NAME Sara Orangetip

FAMILY Whites and Sulphurs

GROUP Whites

COMMON NAMES Falcate Orangetip

FAMILY Whites and Sulphurs

GROUP Whites

The Great Sulphurs. A genus of large butterflies, of a brilliant lemon-yellow or orange-yellow marked with a few darker spots, and with
a narrow band of brown, especially in the
female, on the outer margin of the forewings.
They are very quick in flight. The eggs are
spindle-shaped, acutely pointed, and vertically
ribbed. The caterpillars have a small head, and
are relatively long; the segments of their bodies
resemble beads strung together, the surface
covered with minute papillæ projections in
transverse rows. The chrysalis is concave
dorsally, with a prominently conical head,
the wing-cases compressed, forming a wide
keel-shaped projection on the ventral side.
The genus is mainly tropical. One species,
however, ranges as far north as Long Island
and western Pennsylvania.

Above: *Cloudless Sulphur.* **Right:** *Cloudless Sulphur seeking nectar deep inside a tubular flower.*

Phoebis sennae
▶ Cloudless Sulphur

(Formerly *Catopsilia eubule.*) Wing expanse is
2.50 inches. The caterpillar feeds on legumi-
nous plants, preferably the species of *Cassia*.

COMMON NAME Cloudless Sulphur

FAMILY Whites and Sulphurs

GROUP Sulphurs

Above: *Orange-barred Sulphur is a tropical species occasionally found in south Texas (where photo was taken) and rarely further north..*

This genus is large and is found on every continent except Australia. It is lacking in the very hot tropical regions of both the eastern and western hemispheres, but is found in Greenland, and from there ranging south among the cordilleran uplifts to Patagonia. It is represented from Japan to Norway, and turns up at the Cape of Good Hope.

Phoebis philea
▸ Orange-barred Sulphur

Note: This particular species does not appear in Holland's book but it is representative of its group and the editor has chosen to include it here.

COMMON NAME Orange-barred Sulphur

FAMILY Whites and Sulphurs

GROUP Great Sulphurs

Family

Above: *Large Orange Sulphur.*

Phoebis agarithe
▶ **Large Orange Sulphur**

Note: This particular species does not appear in Holland's book but it is representative of its group and the editor has chosen to include it here.

COMMON NAME Large Orange Sulphur

FAMILY Whites and Sulphurs

GROUP Great Sulphurs

Colias (formerly Meganostoma)
Genus

The Dogface Butterflies. (Note: Holland placed the dogfaces in a genus of their own, although he did acknowledge their relationship to this genus, with which they are now grouped.)

Closely resembling the insects of the next genus (being *Colias*) from which they may be distinguished by the more pointed forewings, and the fact that the rude outlines of the head of a dog are shown in yellow silhouette upon the forewings. There are two species in our territory, one of which, *C. eurydice*, found in California, may be distinguished from the other by the splendid purplish iridescence of the forewings of the male.

Above: *Southern Dogface, upperside showing "poodle" face.*
Right: *Southern Dogface, underside.*

Colias cesonia
▶ Southern Dogface

The sexes are much alike in this species, which ranges from Florida and the Gulf states northward as far as southern Illinois. Wing expanse is 2.25 inches.

COMMON NAME Southern Dogface

FAMILY Whites and Sulphurs

GROUP Dogfaces

The Sulphurs. These are medium-sized but-terflies, yellow, orange, and sometimes white or greenish-yellow with dark-bordered wings, the borders generally heaviest in the female. The eggs are spindle-shaped, vertically and horizontally ribbed, tapering at the top and bottom, and attached to the surface on which they are laid by a flat disk-like expansion. The caterpillars are elongated, with a small head, their bodies generally green, and longitudinally striped. They feed on legumi-nous plants, and especially upon the various species of clover (*Trifolium*) and *Astragalus*, although some boreal species are known to feed on the foliage of huckleberries (*Vaccinium*) and willows.

Colias philodice
▶ Clouded Sulphur

(Formerly Common Sulphur.) This is the common "Puddle-butterfly," or "Clover-but-terfly," many a child has seen gathered in swarms around moist places, or hovering over blossoming clover. There are many varia-tions both in size and color. The females are frequently albinoes, that is to say they are white, rather than yellow. Now and then melanic males turn up, but they are rare. In these the wings are black, of the same color as the borders in normal specimens. Wing expanse is 1.25 to 2.25 inches. The species ranges from Canada to Florida and westward to the Rocky Mountains.

Above: *Clouded Sulphur nectaring on a butterflybush (Buddleia).* **Right:** *Clouded Sulphur nectaring on a mallow flower.*

COMMON NAME Clouded Sulphur

FAMILY Whites and Sulphurs

GROUP Sulphurs

Family

Colias eurytheme
▶ Orange Sulphur

This is a form which is known to be very strongly polymorphic, having many varieties and races. A large winter form has the wings strongly washed with orange; there is a small winter form, which is also washed with orange, though not so strongly. Another form, which belongs to the summer brood, has no orange on the wings, but is plain yellow, and there are still other forms. Wing expanse is 1.60 to 2.15 inches.

The Orange Sulphur has a wide range, extending from the Atlantic to the Pacific, and from Canada to the northern portions of the Gulf states, though not invading the hotter parts of these states.

Above: *Sulphur. Both the Clouded Sulphur and the Orange Sulphur have a similar looking white form of the female.*
Right: *Orange Sulphur nectaring on clover blossom.*

COMMON NAME Orange Sulphur

FAMILY Whites and Sulphurs

GROUP Sulphurs

Eurema (formerly Terias)
Genus

The Yellows. Small butterflies, they are generally some shade of orange or yellow, with wings more delicate in structure than most of the genera belonging to the *Pierinæ* (now *Coliadinæ*). Both wings are rounded, but in a few species they project at the apex of the forewing and at the end of the second median nervule of the hindwing. The eggs are spindle-shaped, and much swollen at the middle. The larva is cylindrical, with a very small head, but the three first segments are larger than those after, which gives the body a humped appearance in front. The chrysalis is compressed laterally, with the wing-cases forming a deep keel on the ventral side, more pronounced than in almost any other American genus.

This is a very large genus, represented by many species in the tropical and subtropical regions of both the eastern and western hemispheres. Many of the species are dimorphic or polymorphic (with two or more forms), and there is a vast deal of confusion as to their classification.

Eurema nicippe
▶ Sleepy Orange

(Formerly *Terias nicippe*, Small Orange.) This species is subject to considerable variation. It is rare in New England, but common south of latitude 40° as far as the Rocky Mountains. It has also been reported from southern California, where it is rare. Wing expanse is 1.50 to 2.00 inches.

Eurema lisa
▶ Little Yellow

(Formerly *Terias lisa*, Little Sulphur.) Allied to other species in the genus, but may be told apart at once by the solid black outer borders of the wings and the absence of the black band on the hind margin of the forewing. Wing expanse is 1.25 to 1.60 inches. Its range is east of the Rockies, from New England to Honduras.

Above right: *The Little Yellow can be recognized by the two black dots near the base of hindwing underside.*
Below right: *Sleepy Orange.*

COMMON NAME Sleepy Orange
FAMILY Whites and Sulphurs
GROUP Sulphurs

COMMON NAME Little Yellow
FAMILY Whites and Sulphurs
GROUP Sulphurs

Family

Eurema daira
▶ Barred Yellow

(Formerly *Terias jucunda*, Fairy Yellow.)
Separable from the preceding species by the
black border surrounding the hindwing, and
the pale under surface. Expanse 1.60 to 1.75
inches. Found in the Gulf states.

Above right: *Barred Yellow. The pale form found in summer.*
Below right: *Barred Yellow. The darker, winter form.*

COMMON NAME Barred Yellow

FAMILY Whites and Sulphurs

GROUP Small Sulphurs

Parnassius
Genus

This peculiar group of butterflies is classed with the *Papilionidæ* because the internal vein of the hindwings is always lacking, a characteristic of all papilionine genera. The caterpillars are not provided with osmeteria, or offensive scent-organs, and pupation takes place upon the ground among loosely scattered leaves which are interwoven by the larva with a few loose strands of silk. The insects are mainly inhabitants of the mountain regions of the northern hemisphere.

Parnassius phoebus
▶ **Phoebus Parnassian**

(Formerly *Parnassius smintheus*, Colorado Parnassian.) This is a somewhat variable species. The caterpillar feeds upon *Sedum* and *Saxifraga*. Male wing expanse is 2.00 to 2.50 inches, that of the female, 2.25 to 3.00 inches. Ranges from New Mexico and Colorado west to California and north to Montana.

Above right: *View of the underside wing of the Phoebus Parnassian on alpine tundra in Denali Park, Alaska.*
Below right: *Upper wing view of the Phoebus Parnassian on alpine tundra in Denali Park, Alaska.*

COMMON NAME Phoebus Parnassian

FAMILY Swallowtails

GROUP Parnassians

Family

The Swallowtails. This great genus has been subdivided for purposes of classification into a number of smaller groups or subgenera, which are useful when dealing with the whole assemblage of species, but which in a manual like this, dealing with only a few forms, may consistently be overlooked.

Eurytides marcellus
▶ Zebra Swallowtail

(Formerly *Papilio ajax*, Papaw Butterfly.) The species is more or less polymorphic (having many forms). The photo represents the form which emerges in the spring of the year from chrysalids which have overwintered. The plate (near right) shows the form which appears in the second brood and in which the tails are much longer than in the first. There are other forms. Wing expanse is 2.50 to 3.25 inches. The caterpillar feeds on the leaves of the Papaw (*Asimina triloba*) and wherever this plant grows the insect may be found. It ranges from New England and Ontario to Florida and far westward through the valley of the Mississippi.

The summer form of Zebra Swallowtail in a plate from the original Holland book.

Right: *Zebra Swallowtail, springtime form.*

COMMON NAME Zebra Swallowtail

FAMILY Swallowtail

GROUP Swallowtails

Papilio glaucus
▶ Eastern Tiger Swallowtail

In the Middle states and southward a large proportion of the females are black, belonging to the form *glaucus*. The dark female form reveals its relationship to the paler form by the stripes on the underside. Sometimes an insect is very black and shows no stripes at all. There can be females with yellow wings on one side and black on the other.

In Ontario and northward and westward to Alaska the females are yellow, like the males. The Alaskan form is very small, dwarfed by the cold and poor feeding. (Note: these are now classified as a species, *Papilio canadensis*, Canadian Tiger Swallowtail.)

The metropolis of the species is the Appalachian uplift; but it ranges northwestward to Alaska and south to the Gulf states. Wing expanse is 3.00 to 5.00 inches. The caterpillars are partial to the foliage of wild cherry trees, but are found on a great variety of plants.

Above: *Eastern Tiger Swallowtail.* **Above right:** *Eastern Tiger Swallowtail dark female form, nectaring on mountain Pieris (Pieris floribunda).* **Below right:** *A common sight is Tiger Swallowtails "puddling" in wet mud, where they are obtaining essential minerals and other nutrients. The old sneaker is clearly providing similar items of value!*

COMMON NAME Eastern Tiger Swallowtail

FAMILY Swallowtail

GROUP Swallowtails

Papilio cresphontes
▶ **Giant Swallowtail**

One of the largest and most showy species of the genus found in our territory. The caterpillar feeds upon *Ptelea*, *Xanthoxylon*, and *Citrus*. It has a wide range from southern Ontario to Florida and through the Mississippi Valley to Mexico. Wing expanse is 3.75 to 5.50 inches.

Papilio troilus
▶ **Spicebush Swallowtail**

The caterpillar, which is green, with two big eye-spots on the back a little behind the head, lives on the foliage of the sassafras and spicebush, where it folds together a leaf in which it conceals itself from view during the daytime, coming out to feed at night. The insect is found throughout the eastern United States and the Mississippi Valley, wherever its food plant occurs. Wing expanse is 3.75 to 4.25 inches.

Above: *The Giant Swallowtail larva greatly resembles a bird dropping. Here shown with "osmeteria" extended. These organs, found in most Swallowtail larvae, produce a smell thought to be distasteful to predators.* **Above right:** *Giant Swallowtail.* **Below right:** *Spicebush Swallowtail puddling in sand after a rainstorm.*

COMMON NAME Giant Swallowtail

FAMILY Swallowtail

GROUP Swallowtails

COMMON NAME Spicebush Swallowtail

FAMILY Swallowtail

GROUP Swallowtails

Papilio
Genus

Papilio polyxenes
▶ Black Swallowtail

(Formerly Eastern Swallowtail.) This butterfly
belongs to a group of the genus that in
England is represented by *P. machaon* of the
fens of Cambridgeshire and Norfolk.

There are many species evidently derived
in past time from common stock, which are
found in America, and the writer believes
that the original centre of dispersion was this
continent, and that the English Swallowtail
represents the most western range of the
migration, which probably began in Tertiary
times, when the horse, the camel, and other
North American animals passed over into
Asia and became subsequently extinct in the
land of their origin. *P. machaon* still exists in
Alaska as the variety *P. aliaska*.

P. polyxenes, is found all over the Atlantic
states and the Mississippi Valley. The caterpillar feeds upon umbelliferous plants, and is
very partial to fennel. Expanse 2.75 to 3.25
inches.

Above right: *Upperwing view of the Black Swallowtail feeding on a thistle.* **Below right:** *View of the underside wing of the Black Swallowtail feeding on a thistle.*

COMMON NAME Black Swallowtail

FAMILY Swallowtail

GROUP Swallowtails

Family

Battus (formerly Papilio)
Genus

Battus philenor
▶ **Pipevine Swallowtail**

The caterpillar feeds upon the foliage of *Aristolochia sipho*, or the "Dutchman's Pipe," a plant extensively grown about verandas and porches, and native to the Allegheny Mountains. It also eats the leaves of *Aristolochia serpentaria*, a smaller plant of the same genus. The wings have an expanse of 3.75 to 4.25 inches. The range is from Massachusetts to California and south into Mexico.

Battus polydamas
▶ **Polydamas Swallowtail**

(Formerly *Papilio polydamus*, Reef Butterfly.) This is the sole representation in our fauna of a great group of splendid butterflies peculiar to the tropics of the New World, which are true papilionids, but without tails, their wings generally of some shade of green, and wonderfully adorned with spots of other colors, generally yellow or crimson. Wing expanse is 3.00 to 3.50 inches. It is found in the extreme southern part of Florida and on the adjoining reefs. It also has a wide range through the Antilles, Mexico, and Central America.

Upperwing view of the Polydamas Swallowtail in a plate from the original Holland book.

Right: *A southern Swallowtail, the Pipevine feeds on plants in the Aristolochiaceae family (including pipevine), and, like the Monarch does by eating milkweed, it incorporates the toxin into its body. The adult is distasteful to birds; it is thought that the Black Swallowtail, Red-spotted Purple, and black form of the Tiger Swallowtail all mimic this distasteful species.*

COMMON NAME Pipevine Swallowtail

FAMILY Swallowtail

GROUP Swallowtails

COMMON NAME Polydamas Swallowtail

FAMILY Swallowtail

GROUP Swallowtails

Family

Urbanus (formerly Eudamus)
Genus

Long-tailed Skippers. The hindwings are more or less elongated at the anal angle in the form of a long tail. There are a number of species found in Central and South America.

Urbanus proteus
▶ Long-tailed Skipper

The caterpillar feeds upon *Wisteria* and various leguminous plants. It is common in Florida, the American tropics, and occasionally found as far north as New York.

Above: *Long-tailed Skipper nectaring on a hawkweed.*

COMMON NAME Long-tailed Skipper

FAMILY Skippers

GROUP Spread-wing Skippers

Epargyreus
Genus

In Skippers, the forewing is generally provided with a costal fold, but never marked with a sexual brand or raised patch of scales on the disk. The antennæ of the *Epargyreus* terminate in a fine point and are bent backward at right angles to the shaft.

Epargyreus clarus
▶ Silver-spotted Skipper

A very common and beautiful insect. The caterpillar usually feeds upon *Robinia* and *Wistaria*. Wing expanse is 1.75 to 2.00 inches. This Skipper has as a wide range, from Quebec to Vancouver Island and south to the Isthmus of Panama.

Above: *Silver-spotted Skipper nectaring on bee balm (Monarda didyma).*

COMMON NAME Silver-spotted Skipper

FAMILY Skippers

GROUP Spread-wing Skippers

Thorybes
Genus

Thorybes bathyllus
▶ Southern Cloudy-wing

(Formerly, Southern Dusky-wing.) This species is distinguished from the preceding species by having larger spots on the forewing that form more of a row, running together almost to a line. Ranges from Connecticut to the Midwest and eastern Texas.

Upperside of the Southern Clowdy-wing in a plate from the original Holland book.

Thorybes pylades
▶ Northern Cloudy-wing

(Formerly, Northern Dusky-wing.) The wings below are a dark brown, shading into gray outwardly. The hindwings are crossed by irregular brown bands, the spots of the upper side reappearing below. Wing expanse is 1.60 inches. Common in New England, westward into Canada and southward to Florida, Texas and Mexico.

Right: *Northern Cloudy-wing sips nectar from butterflyweed (Asclepias tuberosa).*

COMMON NAME Southern Cloudy-wing

FAMILY Skippers

GROUP Cloudy-wing Skippers

COMMON NAME Northern Cloudy-wing

FAMILY Skippers

GROUP Cloudy-wing Skippers

Achalarus
Genus

Achalarus cellus
► Golden-banded Skipper

(Note: now reclassified as *Autocton cellus*, though its common name is the same.) On the upperside the forewings have a golden band that is much brighter and more distinct than in *A. lyciades* and *E. clarus*. This band is echoed on the underside of the forewing, with no silver spots on the hindwings. Wing expanse is 2.00 inches. Found in the Virginias and southward to Arizona and Mexico.

Achalarus lyciades
► Hoary Edge Skipper

Upperside strongly recalls *E. clarus* (Silver-spotted Skipper) but the hoary edge of the hindwings and the absence of the silvery spots found on the hindwings of the Silver-spotted at once separate the two. Wing expanse is 1.65 to 1.95 inches. It is rare in southern New England, common in Southern states as far west as Texas.

Golden-banded Skipper
in a plate from the original Holland book.

Right: *Hoary Edge Skipper male perching on a twig to look for a female.*

COMMON NAME Golden Banded-Skipper

FAMILY Skippers

GROUP Spread-wing Skippers

COMMON NAME Hoary Edge Skipper

FAMILY Skippers

GROUP Spread-wing Skippers

Pyrgus (formerly Hesperia)
Genus

Pyrgus communis
▸ Common Checkered Skipper

(Formerly *Hesperia tessellata*, Tessellated Skipper.) Paler on the underside than on the upperside, with spots enlarged. Wing expanse is 1.00 to 1.35 inches. Ranges from Canada to the Gulf and from the Atlantic to the Pacific.

Pyrgus centaureæ
▸ Grizzled Skipper

Below darker than the preceding species, a white circle at the end of the cell surrounding a black spot, thus forming an eye-like spot; hindwings below light brown scaled with green, crossed by three bands of square spots. Expanse 1.15 inches. Found in northern Europe and Asia and from Alaska to Labrador; extending south on the high mountains both in the West and in the Carolinas.

Above: *Common Checkered Skipper male underside.*
Above right: *Common Checkered Skipper female warming on a rock.* **Below right:** *Common Checkered Skipper. The male is lighter in color than the female and has distinctive blue hairs.*

COMMON NAME Common Checkered Skipper

FAMILY Skippers

GROUP Spread-wing Skippers

COMMON NAME Grizzled Skipper

FAMILY Skippers

GROUP Spread-wing Skippers

Pholisora
Genus

Pholisora catullus
▶ **Common Sootywing**

The caterpillar feeds on "lamb's-quarters" (*Chenopodium*). Wing expanse is 0.80 to 1.15 inches. Ranges over all temperate North America.

Pholisora lybia
(now *Hesperopsis libya*)
▶ **Mohave Sootywing**

Distinguished from the preceding species by the white fringes of the wings and by the markings of the upper side. Wing expanse is 0.80 to 1.40 inches. It is found from western Texas to Nevada and Arizona.

*Mohave Sootywing
in a plate from the original Holland book.*

Right: *The Common Sootywing is common in disturbed places throughout much of the U.S.*

COMMON NAME Common Sootywing

FAMILY Skippers

GROUP Sootywings

COMMON NAME Mohave Sootywing

FAMILY Skippers

GROUP Sootywings

Erynnis (formerly Thanaos)
Genus

Erynnis brizo
▶ **Sleepy Duskywing**

The two rows of light yellow spots on the outer margin of the hindwings appear more distinctly on the underside. The larva feeds on oaks and other plants. Wing expanse is 1.25 to 1.60 inches. Ranges from the Atlantic to the Pacific, from New England to Florida and Arizona.

Erynnis icelus
▶ **Dreamy Duskywing**

The underside is paler than the upper, and marked with many small, indistinct yellow spots, not forming well-defined bands as in the preceding species. The caterpillar feeds on aspen, oaks, and witch-hazel. Wing expanse is 1.00 to 1.20 inches. Ranges from Nova Scotia to Oregon, south to Florida and Arizona.

Above right: *Sleepy Duskywing, a mating pair with the more boldly patterned male on the right.* **Below right:** *Dreamy Duskywing is well camouflaged on a stony path.*

COMMON NAME Sleepy Duskywing

FAMILY Skippers

GROUP Duskywings

COMMON NAME Dreamy Duskywing

FAMILY Skippers

GROUP Duskywings

Erynnis (formerly Thanaos)

Thanaos juvenalis
▶ **Juvenal's Duskywing**

A large species with translucent spots arranged as an interrupted band beyond middle of wing. Wing expanse is 1.35 to 1.60 inches. Its range is from Quebec to Florida and westward to Arizona.

Thanaos funeralis
▶ **Funereal Duskywing**

This species' hindwings are very dark, partly fringed with pure white. Wing expanse is 1.35 inches. Found from western Texas to Mexico.

Above right: *Juvenal's Duskywing is an early spring flier in the eastern U.S.* **Below right:** *Funereal Duskywing's white hindwing border is distinctive.*

COMMON NAMES Juvenal's Duskywing

FAMILY Skippers

GROUP Duskywings

COMMON NAMES Funereal Duskywing

FAMILY Skippers

GROUP Duskywings

Carterocephalus
Genus

Carterocephalus palaemon
► **Arctic Skipper**

(Formerly *Pamphila Mandan.*) This skipper is totally unlike any other species in the fauna. Its wing expanse is 1.10 inches. It is found from Labrador to Alaska, and on the mountains of Idaho and Montana.

Above left: *Arctic Skipper underside showing the silvery markings.* **Above right:** *Arctic Skipper nectaring on dewberry.*

COMMON NAME Arctic Skipper

FAMILY Skippers

GROUP Skipperlings

Ancyloxypha
Genus

Ancyloxypha numitor
▶ Least Skipper

Below, the forewings of this butterfly are black, bordered on the costa and outer margin with a reddish-tan. The hindwings are a pale tan. Wing expanse is 0.75 to 0.95 inch. It ranges from Quebec to Florida and westward to the Rocky Mountains.

Above: *This Least Skipper sips nectar from a chicory flower.*

COMMON NAME Least Skipper

FAMILY Skippers

GROUP Grass Skippers

Hesperia (formerly Erynnis)
Genus

Hesperia uncas
▶ **Uncas' Skipper**

In both sexes, the undersides of the wings are beautifully marked with pearly white spots on a greenish-gray ground. The spots are defined inwardly and outwardly by dark olive shades. Wing expanse is 1.30 to 1.55 inches. It ranges from Pennsylvania to Montana.

Uncas' Skipper in a plate from the original Holland book.

Hesperia leonardus
▶ **Leonard's Skipper**

This skipper is larger than most of the preceding species. Below, the wings are dark brick-red. The spots from the upperside reappear more or less faintly. Wing expanse is 1.25 to 1.35 inches. Its range is from Ontario and New England to Florida, and west throughout the Mississippi Valley.

Left: *Leonard's Skipper, male upperside showing the dark stigma or sex brand in the forewing.* **Right:** *Leonard's Skipper is one of the latest skippers to appear in the summer.*

COMMON NAME Uncas' Skipper

FAMILY Skippers

GROUP Grass Skippers

COMMON NAME Leonard's Skipper

FAMILY Skippers

GROUP Grass Skippers

Family

Above: *A mating pair of Tawny-edged Skippers. The red edge of the male's wing shows on the right.*

Polites themistocles
▶ **Tawny-edged Skipper**

(Formerly *Limochores thaumas*, Fawn-edged Skipper.) Easily distinguished by means of our figures. Below in both sexes wings dull olive with spots of upper side repeated; costa of male edged with red on this side as well as above. Expanse 1.00 to 2.07 inches. Ranges from Canada to the Gulf, west to the Rocky Mountains.

COMMON NAME	Tawny-edged Skipper
FAMILY	Skippers
GROUP	Grass Skippers

Above: *Whirlabout.*

Polites vibex
▸ Whirlabout

(Formerly *Thymelicus brettus.*) This insect,
which is rare in the Northern states, is common in the South and has a wide range
through the American tropics. Wing expanse
1.15 to 1.25 inches.

COMMON NAME Whirlabout

FAMILY Skippers

GROUP Grass Skippers

Polites mystic
▸ Long Dash

(Formerly *Thymelicus mystic.*) The forewings on the underside are tan on the costa near base, the remainder being a dark rust, with the light spots of the upper side repeated, greatly enlarged, pale, and contrasting strongly with the dark ground-color. The hindwings are pale brown on the inner margin. Wing expanse is 1.10 to 1.25 inches. It ranges from southern Canada to Pennsylvania and west to Wisconsin.

Polites peckius
▸ Peck's Skipper

This small species is dark brown below. The light spots of the upperwings reappear here greatly enlarged, especially in the middle of the wings, fused together and pale yellow, contrasting strongly with the rest of the wings. Wing expanse is 1.00 to 1.25 inches. Peck's Skipper ranges from Canada to Virginia west to Kansas and Iowa.

Above: *Peck's Skipper nectaring on tall verbena (Verbena bonariensis).* **Right:** *The Long Dash is often found stealing nectar from blue flag.*

COMMON NAMES Long Dash

FAMILY Skippers

GROUP Grass Skippers

COMMON NAMES Peck's Skipper

FAMILY Skippers

GROUP Grass Skippers

Above: *The male Sachem can be told by the thick dark rectangular mark on his forewing.*

Atalopedes campestris
▸ Sachem

(Formerly *Atalopedes huron.*) Easily distinguished from the figures we give. Wing expanse is 1.15 to 1.35 inches. Ranges from New York to Florida, westward and southwestward into Mexico.

COMMON NAME Sachem

FAMILY Skippers

GROUP Grass Skippers

Above: *Fiery Skipper nectaring on tall verbena (Verbena bonariensis).*

Hylephila phyleus
▶ Fiery Skipper

Wing expanse 1.15 to 1.25 inches. Ranges
from Connecticut to Patagonia everywhere.

COMMON NAME Fiery Skipper

FAMILY Skippers

GROUP Grass Skippers

Above: *Ocola Skipper.*

Panoquina ocola
▸ Ocola Skipper

(Formerly *Prenes ocola*.) This common southern species, which sometimes ranges as far north as the latitude of Pennsylvania, ranges south as far as Bolivia in South America. Expanse 1.45 to 1.60 inches. The specimen here is of the type.

COMMON NAME Ocola Skipper

FAMILY Skippers

GROUP Grass Skippers

Euphyes
Genus

Above: *Dun Skipper.*

Euphyes vestris
▶ Dun Skipper

(Formerly *Euphyes metacomet.*) The markings
of upperside reappear on lowerside, the
ground-color below ranging from pale brown
to purplish-brown. Wing expanse is 1.15 to
1.30 inches. Found from Quebec to the
Carolinas, west to Texas and Alberta and
Assiniboia.

COMMON NAME Dun Skipper

FAMILY Skippers

GROUP Grass Skippers

Pompeius
Genus

Above: *Little Glassywing showing the translucent pale spots in the forewing from which it gets its name.*

Pompeius verna
▶ **Little Glassywing**

(Formerly *Euphyes verna*, Vernal Skipper.)
Below, the wings are paler, inclining to pur-
plish-red. At about the middle of the underside of the hindwings is a semicircle of pale
spots. Wing expanse is 1.15 to 1.35 inches.
Its range is from southern New England to
Virginia, west to Kansas, and north to
Alberta. It is very common in Ohio, Indiana,
and Illinois.

COMMON NAME Little Glassywing

FAMILY Skippers

GROUP Grass Skippers

Poanes (formerly Phycanassa)
Genus

Above: *Broad-winged Skipper.*

Poanes viator
▸ Broad-winged Skipper

(Formerly *Phycanassa viator*.) Below paler than above, the light spots of the upperside reappearing less distinctly; the hindwing traversed from base to middle of outer margin by a light-colored longitudinal ray which is not as plain in the female as in the male. Expanse 1.45 to 1.60 inches. Rare in the Northern states from New Jersey to Wisconsin, but quite abundant in the Southern states as far west as Texas.

COMMON NAME Broad-winged Skipper

FAMILY Skippers

GROUP Grass Skippers

Above: *Hobomok Skipper, the dark form of the female.*

Atrytone hobomok
▶ Hobomok Skipper

In the male, the small apical spots are not enclosed by a band of dark color as in the preceding species, and the pale area on the middle of the hindwings is more restricted, the inner margin of this wing being more widely fuscous. The variety of the female called *pocohontas* by Dr. Scudder is melanic, and is very dark, with conspicuous light spots in the forewing. Wing expanse is 1.25 to 1.50 inches. It ranges from New England, southward and westward over the greater part of the Atlantic region and the valley of the Mississippi.

COMMON NAMES Hobomok Skipper

FAMILY Skippers

GROUP Grass Skippers

Above: *Hobomok Skipper.*

Lerema accius
▶ **Clouded Skipper**

(Formerly Grimy Skipper.) The wings on the underside are smokey dark, clouded with still deeper brown or black. Wing expanse is 1.40 to 1.50 inches. The species occurs from Connecticut to Central America, being quite rare in the north but very common in the hot lands of the south.

Above: *Clouded Skipper feeds at a flower in the pea family.*

COMMON NAME Clouded Skipper

FAMILY Skippers

GROUP Grass Skippers

Classification of North American Butterflies
Occurring North of Mexico
According to North American Butterfly Association, Inc., 2003

Swallowtails — Family Papilionidæ
Parnassians — Subfamily Parnassiinæ
Swallowtails — Subfamily Papilioninæ

Whites and Sulphurs — Family Pieridæ
Whites — Subfamily Pierinæ
Sulphurs — Subfamily Coliadinæ
Mimic-Whites — Subfamily Dismorphiinæ

Gossamer-wing Butterflies — Family Lycaenidæ
Harvesters — Subfamily Miletinæ
Coppers — Subfamily Lycaeninæ
Hairstreaks — Subfamily Theclinæ
Blues — Subfamily Polyommatinæ

Metalmarks — Family Riodinidæ

Brushfooted Butterflies — Family Nymphalidæ
Snouts — Subfamily Libytheinæ
Heliconians and Fritillaries — Subfamily Heliconiinæ
True Brushfoots — Subfamily Nymphalinæ
Admirals and Relatives — Subfamily Limenitidinæ
Leafwings — Subfamily Charaxinæ
Emperors — Subfamily Apaturinae
Morphos — Subfamily Morphinæ
Satyrs — Subfamily Satyrinæ
Clearwings — Subfamily Ithomiinæ
Monarchs — Subfamily Danainæ

Skippers — Family Hesperiidæ
Firetips — Subfamily Pyrrhopyginæ
Spread-wing Skippers — Subfamily Pyrginæ
Skipperlings — Subfamily Heteropterinæ
Grass-Skippers — Subfamily Hesperiinæ
Giant-Skippers — Subfamily Megathyminæ

Glossary

Abdomen the segmented tail area of an insect.

Anal angle the angle along the edge of the wing created by the transition from the outer margin to the inner margin.

Antenna (plural antennae) variously shaped filamentous sensory organs located on the top of the head.

Apex the area of a wing usually furthest from the body.

Base the area of a wing nearest the body.

Club the thickened end of a butterfly's antenna.

Costal margin the front edge of the wing.

Clypeus the hard plate on the top of an insect's head; part of its exoskeleton.

Costa the leading edge of a wing, between the base and the apex.

Coxa (plural coxae) the basal segment of the insect leg, often firmly attached to the body; the hip.

Dorsal on the back.

Exoskeleton a tough external structural body armor (skeleton) made of chitin.

Eye on a butterfly and other insects, consists of two parts. The simple eye (or ocelli) are usually found on the adult insect's head, between its two compound eyes. These focus light from each part of the insect's field of view onto a rhabdome (the equivalent of our retina).

Eye spot a circular eye-like marking found on the wings of some butterflies. In that it looks like the face of a larger animal, can sometimes help to scare away predators.

Femur (plural femora) the third (counting from the body) and often largest segment of the insect leg.

Head the location of the brain, compound eyes, proboscis, pharynx, and point of attachment of the antennae on an insect.

Inner margin the back or trailing edge of the wing.

Labrum the upper "lip" above the butterfly's proboscis.

Margin see outer margin.

Media the fourth major vein in a wing.

Ocelli *see* eye.

Occiput hindmost region on the top of the insect's head.

Outer margin the distal edge of the wing. Also called the termen or margin.

Palpus (plural palpi) one of a pair of appendages on the front of a butterfly's head protecting the proboscis.

Pharynx the front part of the foregut between a butterfly's mouth and esophagus.

Pheromone specific aromatic substances that attract the male and female of a particular species to each other.

Proboscis the long coiled tube through which butterflies feed.

Radius the third major vein in a wing.

Scales flat, variously shaped unicellular outgrowths of the butterfly's exoskeleton

Simple eye *see* eye.

Spiracles a butterfly's breathing pores.

Tarsus (plural tarsi) the last segment of a butterfly's leg, which is equipped with gripping claws and taste organs.

Termen see outer margin.

Thorax an insect's chest area, containing the muscles that allow the legs and wings (also attached to the thorax) to move.

Tibia the fourth segment up on the leg of an insect.

Tornus the corner of a wing where the outer margin meets the inner margin.

Ventral underneath, or on the underside; the belly.

Index

Note: Page numbers in **bold** indicate photographs.

A

Acadian Hairstreak, 112, **113**
Achalarus cellus, 182
Achalarus lyciades, 182
Ageronia feronia. See
    Hamadryas feronia
Agraulis vanillæ, 30
American Copper, 122, **123**
American Lady, 64, **66**, **67**
American Snout, **102**, **103**
Anartia jatrophæ, 70
Anatomy, 7–13
Ancyloxypha numitor, 193
Anthocharis midea, 150
Anthocharis sara, 150
Aphrodite Fritillary, 36, **37**
Appalachian Brown, 90, **91**
Arctic Skipper, **192**
Arrowhead Blue, 138, **139**
Ascia monuste, 140
Asterocampa celtis, 80
Asterocampa clyton, 82
Asterocampa flora, 82
Atalopedes campestris, 200
Atalopedes huron. See
    Atalopedes campestris
Atlantis Fritillary, 38, **39**
Atrytone hobomok, 206
Autocon cellus. See
    Achalarus cellus

B

Baltimore Checkerspot, **42**,
    43

The Banded Elfin. *See*
    Eastern Pine Elfin
Banded Hairstreak, 108, **109**
Barred Yellow, 164, **165**
Battus philenor, 176
Battus polydamas, 176
Black Swallowtail, 174, **175**
Blomfild's Beauty, 84, **85**
Bog Copper, **122**
Boloria bellona, 40
Boloria selene, 40
Bordered Patch, 52, **53**
Branded Purple. *See* White
    Admiral
Brephidium exile, 134
Brephidium isophthalma, 134
Broad-winged Skipper, **205**
Bronze Copper, 124, **125**

C

Cabbage White, 144, **145**
Calephelis perditalis, 104
Callicore clymena, 73
Callophrys gryneus gryneus,
    115
Callophrys henrici, 116
Callophrys irus, 118
Callophrys niphon, 116
Carolina Satyr, 94, **95**
Carterocephalus palaemon,
    192
Cassius Blue, 136, **137**
Caterpillars, 14–16
Catopsilia eubule. See
    Phoebis sennae
Celastrina ladon neglecta, 130
Cercyonis pegala, 100
Checkered White, **142**

Chlorostrymon simæthis, 114
Chlosyne harrisii, 44
Chlosyne janais, 52
Chlosyne lacinia, 52
Chlosyne nycteis, 44
Chrysalids, 16–18
Chrysophanus hypophlœs.
    See *Lycaena phlaeas*
Chrysophanus thoë. See
    Lycaena hyllus
Classification key, 18–24
Clouded Skipper, **208**
Clouded Sulphur, **158**, **159**
Cloudless Sulphur, **152**, **153**
Cœnonympha inornata. See
    Cœnonympha tullia
Cœnonympha tullia, 96
Colias cesonia, 156
Colias eurytheme, 160
Colias philodice, 158
Colorado Parnassian. *See*
    Phoebus Parnassian
Common Alpine, 98, **99**
Common Blue. *See* Summer
    Azure
Common Buckeye, **68**, **69**
Common Checkered-
    Skipper, **184**, **185**
Common Hairstreak. *See*
    Gray Hairstreak
Common Mestra, **72**
Common Ringlet, 96, **97**
Common Snout. *See*
    American Snout
Common Sootywing, 186,
    187
Common Sulphur. *See*
    Clouded Sulphur

Common White. *See*
Checkered White
Common Wood-Nymph,
100, **101**
Compton's Tortoiseshell, 62,
63
Creole Pearly-eye, 88
Crimson-patch, 52
Cuban Crescent, 50
Currant Angel-wing. *See*
Gray Comma
Cystineura amymone. See
Mestra amymone

D
Dainty Sulphur, **148**, **149**
Danaus gilippus, 26
Danaus plexippus, 26
Dreamy Duskywing, 188,
189
Dryas julia, 29
Dun Skipper, **203**
Dwarf Blue. *See* Eastern
Pygmy-blue
Dwarf Yellow. *See* Dainty
Sulphur

E
Eastern Comma, 56, **57**
Eastern Pine Elfin, 116, **117**
Eastern Pygmy-blue, 134
Eastern Swallowtail. *See*
Black Swallowtail
Eastern Tailed Blue, **132**, **133**
Eastern Tiger Swallowtail,
170, **171**
Edwards Hairstreak, **108**
Eggs, 14

Enodia anthedon, 88
Enodia creola, 88
Epargyreus clarus, 179, 182
Erebia discoidalis, 98
Erebia epipsodea, 98
Erynnis brizo, 188
Erynnis icelus, 188
Euchloë genutia. See
Anthocharis midea
Euchloë olympia, 147
Euchloë rosa. See *Euchloë
olympia*
Euphydryas phaeton, 42
Euphyes metacomet. See
Euphyes vestris
Euphyes verna. See *Pompeius
verna*
Euphyes vestris, 203
Euptoieta claudia, 32
Euptoieta hegesia, 32
Eurema daira, 164
Eurema lisa, 162
Eurema nicippe, 162
Eurytides marcellus, 168
Everes amyntula, 132
Everes comyntas, 132
Eyed Brown, **90**

F
Fairy Yellow. *See* Barred
Yellow
Falcate Orangetip, 150, **151**
Fawn-edged Skipper. *See*
Tawny-edged Skipper
Feniseca tarquinius, 120
Field Crescent, 48
Fiery Skipper, **201**
Frosted Elfin, **118**, **119**

Funereal Duskywing, 190,
191

G
Giant Swallowtail, **172**, **173**
Glaucopsyche lygdamus, 138
Glaucopsyche piasus, 138
Golden Banded-Skipper, 182
Grass Nymph. *See*
Appalachian Brown
Gray Comma, **58**, **59**
Gray Hairstreak, **106**, **107**
Great Purple Hairstreak, 110
Great Southern White, **140**,
141
Great Spangled Fritillary, 34,
35
Green Comma, **56**
Grimy Skipper. *See* Clouded
Skipper
Grizzled Skipper, 184
Gulf Fritillary, **30**, **31**

H
Hackberry Emperor, 80, **81**
Hamadryas feronia, 86
Harris' Checkerspot, 44, **45**
Harvester, **120**, **121**
Heliconius charithonia, 28
Henry's Elfin, **116**
Hermeuptychia sosybius. See
Neonympha sosybius
Hesperia leonardus, 194
Hesperia tessellata. See
Pyrgus communis
Hesperia uncas, 194
Hesperopsis libya, 186
Hoary Edge, 182, **183**

Hoary Elfin. *See* Frosted Elfin
Hobomok Skipper, **206,**
  207
Hunter's Butterfly, 64, 66
Hydaspe Fritillary, 38
Hylephilahy phyleus, 201

I
Imagos, 18, 19–24

J
Julia Heliconian, **29**
Junonia cœnia, 68
Juvenal's Duskywing, 190,
  191

K
Karner Melissa, **128**, **129**
Karwinski's Beauty, 84
Keys, classification, 18–24

L
Large Orange Sulphur, **155**
Least Copper. *See* Bog
  Copper
Least Skipper, **193**
Leonard's Skipper, **194**, **195**
Leopard-spot, **73**
Leptotes cassius, 136
Leptotes marina, 136
Lerema accius, 208
Libytheana carinenta, 102
Life cycle, 14–18
Limenitis archippus, 78
Limenitis arthemis arthemis,
  76
Limenitis arthemis astyanax,
  74, 76

Limenitis disippus. See
  Limenitis archippus
Limenitis weidemeyerii, 76
Limochores thaumas. See
  Polites themistocles
Little Glassywing, **204**
Little Sulphur. *See* Little
  Yellow
Little Wood-satyr, 92, **93**
Little Yellow, 162, **163**
Long Dash, 198, **199**
Long-tailed Skipper, **178**
Lucas' Orange-tip. *See* Sara
  Orangetip
Lycaeides melissa, 126, 128
Lycaeides melissa samuelis,
  128
Lycaena epixanthe, 122
Lycaena helloides, 124
Lycaena hyllus, 124
Lycaena phlaeas, 122
Lycœna heteronea. See
  Glaucopsyche piasus
Lycœna melissa. See
  Lycaeides melissa
Lycœna pseudargiolus. See
  Celastrina ladon neglecta
Lycœna scudderi. See
  Lycaeides melissa
  samuelis
Lycœna theona. See *Leptotes*
  cassius

M
Marine Blue, 136, **137**
Meadow Crescent. *See* Field
  Crescent
Meadow Fritillary, 40, **41**

Megisto cymela, 92
Megisto rubricata, 94
Melanis pixe, 105
Melissa Blue, 126, **127**
Mestra amymone, 72
Mexican Fritillary, 32
Milbert's Tortoiseshell, 62, **63**
Mohave Sootywing, 186
Monarch, 26, **27**, 74, 78
Mountain Silverspot. *See*
  Atlantis Fritillary
Mourning Cloak, **60**, **61**
Mustard White, **143**

N
Nathalis iole, 148
Neonympha eurytus. See
  Megisto cymela
Neonympha rubricata, 94
Neonympha sosybius, 94
North American butterflies,
  209
Northern Cloudy-wing, 180,
  181
Northern Dusky-wing. *See*
  Northern Cloudy-wing
Northern Pearly-eye, 88, **89**
Nymphalis antiopa, 60
Nymphalis californica, 62
Nymphalis j-album. See
  Nymphalis vaualbum
Nymphalis milberti, 62
Nymphalis vaualbum, 62

O
Ocola Skipper, **202**
"Olive" Juniper Hairstreak,
  115

Olympia Marble, **147**

Orange-barred Sulphur, **154**

Orange Sulphur, **160**, **161**

Oreas Comma, 56

P

Painted Crescent, 48

Painted Lady, **66**

Pamphila mandan. See
Carterocephalus
palaemon

Panoquina ocola, 202

Papaw Butterfly. *See* Zebra
Swallowtail

Papilio ajax. See *Eurytides*
marcellus

Papilio aliaska, 174

Papilio asterias, 174

Papilio asterius, 174

Papilio cresphontes, 172

Papilio glaucus, 170

Papilio machaon, 174

Papilio polydamus. See
Battus polydamas

Papilio polyxenes, 174

Papilio troilus, 172

Parnassius phoebus, 166

Parnassius smintheus. See
Parnassius phoebus

Pearl Crescent, 46, **47**

Peck's Skipper, **198**

Phaeon Crescent, **48**, **49**

Phoebis agarithe, 155

Phoebis philea, 154

Phoebis sennae, 152

Phoebus Parnassian, 166, **167**

Pholisora catullus, 186

Pholisora lybia, 186

Phycanassa viator. See
Poanes viator

Phyciodes campestris, 48

Phyciodes frisia, 50

Phyciodes nycteis. See
Chlosyne nycteis

Phyciodes phaon, 48

Phyciodes picta, 48

Phyciodes pratensis. See
Phyciodes campestris

Phycoides texana, 50

Phyciodes tharos, 46

Pieris napi, 143

Pieris protodice. See *Pontia*
protodice

Pieris rapœ, 144

Pieris virginiensis, 146

Pipevine Swallowtail, 176,
177

Plain Ringlet. *See* Common
Ringlet

Poanes viator, 205

Poey's Crescent. *See* Cuban
Crescent

Polites mystic, 198

Polites peckius, 198

Polites themistocles, 196

Polites vibex, 197

Polydamas Swallowtail, 176

Polygonia comma, 56

Polygonia faunus, 56

Polygonia interrogationis, 54

Polygonia progne, 58

Pompeius verna, 204

Pontia protodice, 142

Prenes ocola. See *Panoquina*
ocola

Pupae, 16–18

Purplish Copper, 124, **125**

Pygmy Blue. *See* Western
Pygmy-blue

Pyrameis huntera, 64, 66

Pyrgus centaureœ, 184

Pyrgus communis, 184

Q

Queen, 26, **27**

Question Mark, 54, **55**

R

Red Admiral, 64, **65**

Red-bordered Pixie, **105**

Red-disked Alpine, 98

Red Emperor, 82

Red Satyr, 94

Red-spotted Purple, 74, **75**

Red-streaked Alpine. *See*
Red-disked Alpine

Reef Butterfly. *See*
Polydamas Swallowtail

Rosy Marble-wing. *See*
Olympia Marble

Rounded Metalmark, **104**

S

Sachem, **200**

Sara Orangetip, 150, **151**

Satyrium acadica, 112

Satyrium calanus, 108

Satyrium edwardsii, 108

Satyrium liparops, 112

Satyrodes appalachia, 90

Satyrodes canthus. See
Satyrodes appalachia

Satyrodes eurydice, 90

Scudder's Blue. *See* Karner Melissa

Silver-banded Hairstreak, **114**

Silver-bordered Fritillary, 40

Silver-spotted Skipper, **179**, 182

Silvery Blue, 138, **139**

Silvery Checkerspot, 44

Sleepy Duskywing, 188, **189**

Sleepy Orange, 162, **163**

Small Orange. *See* Sleepy Orange

Smyrna blomfildia, 84

Smyrna karwinskii, 84

Southern Cloudy-wing, 180

Southern Dogface, **156**, **157**

Southern Dusky-wing. *See* Southern Cloudy-wing

Southern Wood-nymph. *See* Common Wood-nymph

Speyeria aphrodite, 36

Speyeria atlantis, 38

Speyeria cybele, 34, 36

Speyeria rhodope, 38

Spicebush Swallowtail, 172, **173**

Striped Hairstreak, 112, **113**

Strymon melinus, 106

Subfamily key, 18

Summer Azure, 130, **131**

T

Tawny-edged Skipper, **196**

Tawny Emperor, 82, **83**

Terias jucunda. See *Eurema daira*

Terias lisa. See *Eurema lisa*

Terias nicippe. See *Eurema nicippe*

Tessellated Skipper. *See* Common Checkered-Skipper

Texan Crescent, 50, **51**

Texas Bagvein. *See* Common Mestra

Thanaos funeralis, 190

Thanaos juvenalis, 190

Thecla damon. See *Callophrys gryneus gryneus*

Thecla edwardsi. See *Satyrium edwardsii*

Thecla halesus, 110

Thecla henrici. See *Callophrys henrici*

Thecla irus. See *Callophrys irus*

Thecla m-album, 110

Thecla melanus. See *Strymon melinus*

Thecla niphon. See *Callophrys niphon*

Thecla simœthis. See *Chlorostrymon simœthis*

Thistle Butterfly, **66**

Thorybes bathyllus, 180

Thorybes pylades, 180

Thymelicus brettus. See *Polites vibex*

Thymelicus mystic. See *Polites mystic*

U

Uncas' Skipper, 194

Urbanus proteus, 178

V

Vanessa atalanta, 64

Vanessa cardui, 64, 66

Vanessa virginiensis, 66

Variable Cracker, 86, **87**

Varied Blue. *See* Arrowhead Blue

Variegated Fritillary, **32**, **33**

Vernal Skipper. *See* Little Glassywing

Viceroy, 74, **78**, **79**

W

Western Pygmy-blue, 134, **135**

Western Tailed Blue, **132**, **133**

West Virginia White, **146**

Whirlabout, **197**

White Admiral, 74, **76**, **77**

White-M Hairstreak, 110, **111**

White Peacock, 70, **71**

White-skirted Calico. *See* Variable Cracker

Z

Zebra Heliconian, **28**

Zebra Swallowtail, 168, **169**

Photo Credits

Steven Daniel: American Snout, 103;; Applachian Brown, 91; Atlantis Fritillary, 39; Baltimore Checkerspot pupa, 43; Banded Hairstreak, 109; Black Swallowtail (all), 175; Blomfild's Beauty, 85; Bog Copper, 122; Bordered Patch, 53; Broad-winged Skipper, 205; Cabbage White female, 145; Cassius Blue, 137; Checkered White, 142; Cloudless Sulphur, 153; Common Alpine (all), 99; Common Buckeye on sand, 69; Common Mestra, 72; Common Ringlet, 97; Common Sootywing, 187; Compton Tortoiseshell, 63; Dainty Sulphur (all), 148; Dun Skipper, 203; Eastern Tailed Blue,133; Eighty-eight or Leopard Spot, 73; Funereal Duskywing, 191; Giant Swallowtail larva, 172; Gray Comma, 25, 59; Gray Comma underside, 58; Great Southern White, 140; Great Spangled Fritillary on zinnia, 35; Gulf Fritillary larva, 31; Harris' Checkerspot on hawkweed, 45; Henry's Elfin, 116; Hobomok Skipper, 207; Julia Longwing, 29; Juniper Hairstreak, 115; Juvenal's Duskywing, 191; Large Orange Sulphur, 155; Leonard's Skipper, 195; Little Wood Satyr, 93; Little Yellow, 162; Long Dash, 199; Marine Blue, 137; Meadow Fritillary, 41; Melissa Blue, 127; Mourning Cloak, 61; Mustard White, 143; Northern Pearly Eye, (all) 89; Ocola Skipper, 202; Olympia Marble, 147; Orange-barred Sulphur, 154; Painted Lady, 66; Pearl Crescent on rock, 47; Phaon Crescent (underside), 49; Phoebus Parnassian (all), 167; Pipevine Swallowtail, 177; Purplish Copper, 125; Question Mark, 55; Question Mark underside, 55; Red Admiral (head down), 64; Red-bordered Pixie, 105; Rounded Metalmark, 104; Sachem, 200; Silver Banded Hairstreak, 114; Silvery Blue, 139; Sleepy Orange, 163; Southern Dogface, 156, 157; Tawny Emperor "sunning," 83; Tawny Emperors mating, 83; Tawny-edged Skipper, 196; Texan Crescent (all), 51; Tiger Swallowtails "puddling," 171; Variable Cracker, 87; Variegated Fritillary, 33; Viceroy, 79; Viceroy larva, 78; Western Pygmy-blue (all), 135; Western Tailed Blue, 132, 133; Whirlabout, 197; White Admiral, 76; White M Hairstreak, 111; White Peacocks mating, 71; Zebra Longwing, 28.

Carol A. Southby: Cabbage White, 145; Clouded Sulphur, 158; Common Buckeye, 69; Common Checkered Skipper female, 185; Common Checkered Skipper male, 185; Common Checkered Skipper male (underside), 184; Eastern Tailed Blue (underside), 132; Eastern Tiger Swallowtail, 170; Edwards' Hairstreak, 108; Fiery Skipper, 201; Frosted Elfin female, 119; Frosted Elfin male, 118; Gray Hairstreak on knapweed, 107; Hackberry Emperor, 81; 'Karner' Melissa Blue, 129, 128; Orange Sulphur, 161; Peck's Skipper, 198; Silvery Blue (upperside), 139.

David T. Southby: Acadian Hairstreak, 113; American Copper, 123; American Lady, 66; American Lady, 67; American Snout (upperside), 102; Aphrodite Fritillary (all), 37; Arctic Skipper, 192; Arctic Skipper (underside), 192; Atlantis Fritillary (upperside), 39; Baltimore Checkerspot (upper/underwings), 42, 43; Barred Yellow (all),165; Bronze Copper, 125; Carolina Satyr, 95; Clouded Skipper, 208; Clouded Sulphur, 159; Cloudless Sulphur, 152; Common Buckeye (underside), 68; Common Wood Nymph, 101; Dreamy Duskywing, 189;

Eastern Comma (underside), 57; Eastern Comma, 57; Eastern Pine Elfin, 117; Eastern Tiger Swallowtail, (dark female), 171; Eyed Brown, 90; Falcate Orangetip, 151; Giant Swallowtail, 173; Gray Hairstreak,106; Great Southern White female, 141; Great Spangled Fritillary on butterflyweed, 35; Green Comma, 56; Gulf Fritillary, 30, 31; Harris' Checkerspot on daisy, 45; Harvester (all), 121; Hoary Edge Skipper, 183; Hobomok Skipper, 206; Least Skipper, 193; Leonard's Skipper,194; Little Glassywing, 204; Long-tailed Skipper, 178; Mating Pearl Crescents,47; Meadow Fritillary on goldenrod, 41; Milbert's Tortoiseshell, 63; Monarchs, 27; Mourning Cloak (underside), 60; Northern Cloudywing, 181; Phaon Crescent, 48; Queen, 27; Red Admiral nectaring, 65; Red-spotted Purple (underside), 75; Red-spotted Purple, 75; Sara Orangetip, 151; Silver-spotted Skipper, 179; Sleepy Duskywing, 189; Spicebush Swallowtail,173; Striped Hairstreak, 113; Sulphur, white form female, 160; Summer Azure,131; Variegated Fritillary, 32; Viceroy on Queen Anne's lace, 79; West Virginia White, 146; White Admiral nectaring,77; Zebra Swallowtail, 169.

BUTTERFLY SIGHTINGS

Species	Location	Observations

BUTTERFLY SIGHTINGS

Species	Location	Observations

BUTTERFLY SIGHTINGS

Species	Location	Observations

BUTTERFLY SIGHTINGS

Species	Location	Observations

BUTTERFLY SIGHTINGS

Species	Location	Observations